Witches

Olga Hoyt

WITCHES

Abelard-Schuman
London • New York • Toronto

LONDON	NEW YORK	TORONTO
Abelard-Schuman	Abelard-Schuman	Abelard-Schuman
Limited	Limited	Canada Limited
8 King St. WC2	257 Park Ave. S.	200 Yorkland Blvd.
	10010	425

An Intext Publisher

Printed in the United States of America

Contents

Acknowledgments

The author and publisher wish to thank the following for permission to use the illustrations listed below:

British Museum for the pictures on pages 75, 90, 101, 129, and 143.
Freethought Press Association for the picture on page 102.
George G. Harrap & Company Ltd. for the pictures from *Witchcraft, Magic and Alchemy* by Grillot de Givry and Emile Angelo, which appear on pages 24, 32, 41, 45, 50, 51,

52, 72, 74, 97, 109, 111, 114, 122, 123.

D.C. Heath and Company for the picture from *Man's Work and World, A History of Industry* by Eleanor Perret (1935), which appears on page 79.

Leipzig Museum for the picture on page 34.

Opera News for the picture on page 77.

The Prado for the picture on page 30.

Grateful acknowledgment is also made to the New York Public Library for illustrations from its picture collection.

O. H.

Illustrations

Introduction

The habits and practices of witches seem almost unbeliev-
able to us today, but starting from the early days of
recorded history men and women have believed in magic
and supernatural powers. Compared to later witches who
were accused of doing evil, following the bidding of a
creature they called Satan, early witches were innocents,
with their healings and readings of the stars. As the
practices of the witches became more diabolical, the in-
tensity of their persecution increased. Then, too, there were

periods when government and church hounded all those who did not believe as they did.

This book attempts to give a glimpse of some of the activities—both real and imagined—of witches and of how they were punished, whether they were guilty as accused or not. It is not a scholarly study of the witchcraft cult, but rather a sampling of black magic as practiced through the ages. Though the witches' deeds were often grisly, an account of them may be instructive as reflecting the temper of the times. Man has always had a spirited imagination; how this was fostered by the belief in the supernatural is chronicled in these pages.

The reader should keep in mind the background of the events described, to understand them fully. For example, the wild occasion of the Sabbat as practiced by the witches has no connection with our modern Sabbath. In including astrologers among those who practiced witchcraft, it must be remembered that witches used astrology as a tool of magic, but that one did not have to be a witch to dabble in astrology. Many reputable astronomers were also astrologists without being witches.

Let us, then, step back through the pages of history and view witchcraft as it *did* occur. You may find it instructive and interesting.

Part I
The Habits of
Witches

The picture of the witch—dressed in flowing black and a tall pointed hat, streaking through the darkening skies astride a broomstick, cackling and chortling—has long been associated with fairy tales and Halloween. The witch had a jet-black cat and with her long bony fingers she stirred poisonous brews of herbs and toads in her cauldron.

Long before the birth of Christ the powers of witches were believed by many to be real. The deeds and the habits of these witches were far more horrifying than those of any of our popular witches of today.

From the pre-Christian times of the early Greeks—who had been nurtured on a diet of literature filled with myths and legends—horror, fear and suspicion helped foster the belief that living persons had magical powers, that sorceresses could draw down the moon from the skies, that men could be transformed into beasts.

Tragically, the witch cult of the ancient world persisted, though changed and influenced by the acceptance of Christianity. The cult grew through the years into such a monstrous delusion that thousands of people accused of being witches were tortured, beheaded and burned in the sixteenth and seventeenth centuries in Europe, before the madness was cleared from men's minds.

Each age and each region of the world had its own witches, each with particular magical practices. Some cast spells, some put pins in wax images, some poisoned, some predicted, some uttered incantations.

In France and England the witches were believed to have traveled by broomstick; in Italy and Spain the Devil (in the shape of a goat) transported them. Some were said to fly after the application of an ointment concocted of strong boiled herbs and the fat of little children.

The earliest reports of witchcraft and magic-making came to us as legends or myths. It would be impossible to date the earliest sorceress or her rites. The ancients believed that everyone—men and women, old or young and beautiful—was considered capable of possessing magical powers. After all, gods and goddesses had been worshipped for centuries, and so ordinary worshippers accepted easily the god who revealed himself as an animal. For example, a dancing horned figure wearing a stag's head was found on the wall of a cave used in the Stone Age.

One very old property of witches, which has always been of prime importance, is the wax image. Probably no

Typical witch flying on broomstick, as drawn by Maxfield Parrish

Witches brewing a charm (from woodcut in Ulrich's Witches, Augsburg, 1508)

other single item is encountered so frequently in the records of witches, in all ages and all countries. Such figures, it is known, were used even in earliest Egypt. One story dates back to a king, Neb-ahu-Ra, of the Third Dynasty, about 3830 B.C. One of the king's high officials, Aba-aner, was greatly upset when he discovered that his wife was attracted to a soldier of the royal guard. Aba-aner made a crocodile of wax, took it to the river and recited several spells, commanding the crocodile to seize the soldier when he saw him in the river. The wax crocodile was thrown into the river, where magically it came to life, a twelve-foot-long creature. The soldier went swimming, was clasped by the jaws of the crocodile, who, at Aba-aner's order, disappeared with its victim in the depths of the Nile. The guilty wife was punished with death by the king, who apparently approved of the magic.

The Egyptian Pharaoh Rameses III discovered that a certain high official, Hui, was involved in a conspiracy against him. According to the records of the trials, Hui went to the royal library and took out a book of spells. Then he made little figures of wax, representing men he wished to harm, including the king. Hui was accused of carrying out all the "horrible things and all the wickednesses which his heart could imagine." The judges compelled him to commit suicide.

The use of wax figures passed then from ancient Egypt to Greece, and then to Rome, from which it finally came to western Europe. In Scotland in the seventh century the wax image was used for the same purpose, to bring evil to the one the figure represented. The perpetrators, called *witches*, were punished by death.

King Duffus had enemies. "A company of hags roasted his image made of wax upon a wooden spit, reciting certain words of enchantment, and basting the figure with a poisonous liquor. These, when apprehended, declared that as the wax melted, the body of the king should decay." The wax figure was destroyed, the king did not die and the witches were burned.

By this time in the ancient world, witchcraft, or magic, was already considered to be of two types—black and white. The black kind was done with some sort of connection with an unseen power, some liaison with the Devil's servants. White magic could be used for curing warts or insuring safe travel at sea.

Magic was also used for political purposes. Wizards, wise men and priests of Greece and Rome were respected. Because of their communion with the gods, it was said, they could advise about the future. They chanted incantations, healed, advised and directed. In addition, it was said they could control the wind and turn human beings into animals. A lesser group of these wizards were the commercial "quacks." They fashioned potions and poisons, but whatever they did they did for money.

In Greece and Rome, astrology was allied with witchcraft. The astrologers, or fortune-tellers, cast spells and made predictions. Perhaps they were called upon to damage crops and vines, to give sickness to the cattle. Often pre-

Sorcerer riding on a goat

dictions were made about the death of a ruler—all to the advantage of his opponents. In the fifth century B.C., laws were passed, punishing with death wicked witches who cast malevolent spells. And in 139 B.C. came an edict that all sorcerers would have to leave Rome. But the law came to nothing. The charlatans flocked back to an eager paying public who believed in them.

Witches were often men. However, the Greeks and Romans did not lack their share of female witches, who could be mysterious and lovely, or horrid hags capable of the most diabolical acts. In Thessaly, in northern Greece, lived a group of sorceresses who were the terror of the people. These witches were constantly trying to draw the moon down from the skies, and they spent much of their time making herb concoctions. In bare feet, their hair hanging down, their robes tucked up around their waists, they gathered bones and herbs—often in a cemetery by the light of the full moon. Perhaps the most famous of these witches was the Crone of Thessaly, Erichtho, described by Lucan in his *Pharsalia*.

Erichtho was sought out by Sextus, the son of Pompey (106-48 B.C.), who wanted to know about the future of the Romans. Erichtho lived in a grave from which the ghost of the dead had been expelled. She was pale, lean and ugly, with tangled, matted hair. Her powers were immense. She could revive the dead. She could kill anyone.

One night Sextus set out with some friends to find Erichtho. They went into the graveyard. Past deserted graves, they found her busy collecting magical herbs. Sextus beseeched her to divulge what the Fates had in store, or to turn aside what the Fates were going to bring, so that he would have no doubts about the future. "Extort this secret from the gods, or force the dead to confess what they know," he said.

The crone protested that she could not break the chain of fate, but she agreed to get news of the future for Sextus. Then the witch's work began. After searching a field of battle, Erichtho, scattering the wolves before her, found just what she wanted. She put on a robe, covered her face with her hair and arranged a wreath of vipers around her head. Then from her supplies she took such items as the froth from the jaws of a mad dog and used them. Then she chanted her incantations, which sounded like the barking of a dog and the howl of a wolf, the hooting of a screech owl, the yells of a wild beast and the hiss of serpents. It was a long, noisy, frightening chant demanding the ghost of the dead. His spirit appeared. Erichtho commanded the spirit to speak, promising him that if he told her what she wanted to know, he would never again be subject to any magician. The spirit gave the wanted information. Then Erichtho used herbs and more magic to construct a funeral pyre. The spirit placed himself on the pyre, the crone applied the torch and the spirit burned.

Such, we are told, were the habits of one of the most notorious witches of ancient times.

In the second century A.D. a Roman who had lived in Africa, Lucius Apuleius, wrote one of the most famous and widely read books of his time, the popularity of which later helped bring him to the courts, accused of sorcery. *Metamorphoses*, or *The Golden Ass*, was a romance, to be sure, but it also made the hateful operations of witchcraft more believable to the book's readers. Apuleius described a witch thus: "She can call down the sky, hang earth in heaven, freeze fountains, melt mountains, raise the spirits of the dead, send gods to hell. . . ."

He added a note of levity when describing further acts of the witch: "She turned a neighboring innkeeper, whose

Medea, using magic, rejuvenates Aeson (from engraving by J.W. Bauer; 17th century)

competition damaged her trade, into a frog and now the poor old fellow swims about in a vat of his own wine and, squatting deep in the lees, summons his former customers with hoarse, importunate croak."

The book ended in mysticism. Later, Apuleius was accused by his wife's relatives of immorality and sorcery, of having used magic to persuade his wife to marry him and to give him property. The case was considered in all seriousness and tried before Claudius Maximus, around 155-161 A.D. Apuleius' defense was explained in his work, *Apologia*, in which he expressed the principle that there were certain divine powers, midway between gods and men, from whom all divination and magic came. However, Apuleius was not on trial for his beliefs, but rather on the specific charge of practicing magic. One of the charges was that he bribed fishermen to bring him certain curious fish for his spells. (Apuleius replied to this charge by declaring that fish were not mentioned in the magical authorities as having any value.) He was also accused of having bewitched, with magical incantation, a boy who was reported to have gone mad. Apuleius countered by saying that if he had practiced a rite "mysterious, loathsome, horrible," would he have allowed fifteen slaves to be present? Apuleius *did* believe in a "communion of speech" that set men in touch with divine things; but he proved he was innocent of sorcery.

The Romans recognized the two forms of magic, white and black. White magic had for centuries been a sure shield against misfortune and enchantment, practiced not only by white witches, but even by housewives who had their own system of charms to protect them when they could not get professional help.

White magic was tolerated. Not so with black magic. With the coming of Christianity, the Church, along with the populace, admitted the existence of witches, and declared that they were evil, but in the early years it did not punish black witches severely. Those who were faithful Christians knew that magic was doomed to failure since it was outside the pattern of belief in God. It was only in later years, when the Church felt witchcraft was allied with heresy and was competing with it for adherents, that it took a stronger position.

Black witches were feared, as all such witches have been through the ages, and many of their reported practices —carry-overs, to be sure, from primitive times—were to be seen in witch activities of many years later. The witches would gather for their big festivals at the full moon, naked or in black robes, to pick herbs at midnight. They danced, and howled, and shouted nonsense rhymes. They tore a black lamb into pieces to summon the dead. On the 15th of February they held special celebrations to which witches came from far and near.

Young men covered their bodies with goatskins as they danced. Goats were sacrificed and women were whipped with straps made from hides. Spells were cast on enemies. Masks were worn. Poisons were made from vile animal substances. Pins were stuck into images, or the images were burned. Animal symbolism was prominent, as it was to be for centuries, and as it had been for centuries. The witches howled like wolves, wearing wolf masks. The horned goat was there, too.

When Christianity grew strong it complicated its views on witchcraft. Many of the old mysterious beliefs of paganism found their way into the Christian belief, but beginning about the third century the Church realized that many of the witches who were "devil's servants" doing "devil's work" were renouncing God in their magic. (One part of the witches' ritual was chanting the Lord's Prayer backward.)

As the Church kept an eye on black witches, the

Goat worship (from a fresco by Goya in the Prado, Madrid)

Roman emperors clung to their belief in seers, sorcery and astrologers. Although from time to time they publicly banned them, they personally continued to put great faith in them. Emperor Augustus believed in lucky and unlucky days. Nero anxiously consulted an astrologer, although he claimed he did not believe in occultists. As much as charlatans and magic-doers, with their love potions, their incantations and charms, were laughed at by critics, magic still had a devastating hold on the people.

One of its most vile aspects was the use of human sacrifice to divine the future. It was thought that by the sacrifice of humans a bribe was given whereby the true decrees of the fates could be secured from the unseen powers. Commodus (180-92 A.D.) ordered young boys selected for sacrifice, on the theory that by examining the human entrails, the future could be discovered. Caracalla, who reigned from 211 to 217, practiced the same art, ordering handsome and noble youths slain. Maxentius (306-12) and Julian (361-63) were persuaded by various magicians to do the same. One emperor, Septimus Severus (193-211) condemned many fortune-tellers to death, as well as executing those who had consulted them. Yet, twenty-five years later, Alexander Severus was helping astrologers and magicians with gifts of money. By the fourth century, several emperors were forbidding sacrifices at night, which indicated that they were still celebrated.

Rome, of course, was not the only place where witchcraft flourished. In England, in the seventh century, the Archbishop of Canterbury composed laws regulating punishments for magical practices and ceremonies. These punishments for consorting with the Devil and his work were not severe: do penance, fast or spend some days in prison. But the laws indicate what the witches of the day were up to. The ones to be punished were those who "goeth about in the masque of a stag or a bull-calf . . . those who by their craft raise storms . . . sacrifices to demons . . . consulteth soothsayers who divine by birds . . .. If any woman hath placed her son or daughter upon the house-top or in the oven in order to ensure them health. . . ." It was bread and water for three years for anyone who "hath vowed a vow and hath fulfilled the same at a clump of trees, or a spring of water, or at certain rocks. . . ." For anyone who transformed himself into the appearance of a wild animal, it was three years of penance, for such transformation was considered a devilish practice. It was known that the Demon could be a bull or a huge black ram, while his

A witch causing a monster to appear

servants favored the shape of a cat. Thus the person who assumed an animal disguise or mask was, in essence, putting himself somehow in contact with the Devil.

In France, witchcraft was much the same. The Salic Law in the fifth century established various fines for witchcraft: for launching a mortal curse or fashioning the witch's knot, or defaming a man as a wizard—all were punished by a fine of seventy-two sous and half a golden coin. Any witch convicted of having eaten human flesh had to give up two hundred sous.

Witches continued to trouble their neighbors by invoking devils, bewitching drinking horns, brewing philtres, sending hailstorms, foretelling future events, and, if they were really wicked, transferring their allegiance to Satan.

During these years in Europe, the Christian Church continued to try to stamp out superstition and the magic that went along with it, but it was difficult, for the masses had a heritage of centuries of mysticism in pagan belief. As they did not relinquish their belief in witchcraft, but indeed became more and more convinced that demons abounded everywhere, the laws against witches in many countries became more severe. Certain monks in France acquired notoriety as magicians. The witches there in the eleventh century, during the reign of Robert the Good, included a number of clerics. Around 1000 A.D. a band of sorcerers used to meet at Orléans on certain nights in a lonely and deserted house. Each one arrived with a lantern in his hand. As they gathered together, they extinguished the lights, invoked Satan and other devils, and gave themselves over to orgies. As they lay in prison, after being caught at their terrible deeds, they were beseeched to reform, but to no avail. They were sent to the stake and burned.

By the twelfth century it was obvious that government and Church edicts had not stamped out witchcraft. The Christian Church at Rome began to take even stronger measures. In the next centuries the practice of witchcraft became closely identified with heresy against the Church, and as the persecutions increased so, ironically, did belief in the actual powers of the witches.

By the beginning of the fourteenth century the Church was convinced, largely through the findings of the Inquisition, that sorcery involved a personal pact with Satan, and therefore *was* heresy of the vilest kind. The pact was now considered an essential preliminary to the practice of witchcraft. Now, too, came the horror stories of the witches' secret meetings, or Sabbats, where God was renounced Satan was adored and black magic was practiced. It was unfortunate that many of those who held beliefs that were

A witch preparing a philtre (by unknown master of the Flemish School; mid-fifteenth century)

not the beliefs of the official Church became responsible for the beginnings of the witch mania in the fifteenth century, a mania that culminated in the terrors of the sixteenth and seventeenth century witch-hunts and persecutions.

Beginning even in the twelfth century, heretics—those who did not adhere to Church doctrine—held secret gatherings, "heretics' Sabbaths," to celebrate their own rites. By the beginning of the thirteenth century the largest of these groups were the Albigenses of the south of France. But there were many other such groups throughout Europe, in France, Germany and Italy. Popular talk began to attribute all kinds of orgies to these meetings. The Catharists, in the twelfth century, were accused of Devil-worship, sorcery, immorality, grave-robbing, cannibalism and magical flight. The rise of the Inquisition, which was to deal with the evil of heresy, helped to further the identification of heresy with witchcraft, and the heretics' Sabbaths seemed to become as one with the black witches' Sabbats.

Witches were real people in Europe and England during the Middle Ages. They were not just the products of imagination, fear or superstition. As the Inquisition proceeded, witches were examined and questioned. Their testimonies, whether or not they were colored by exaggeration and neurotic fantasy or were the result of torture, indicate that witches believed in their own powers and confessed to belonging to the subversive organizations. It has been established that much of what the witches claimed really *did* occur. If a witch asserted she had consorted with the Devil—she had. But the Devil to her was the leader of her group (the coven), who was personifying the Devil.

The pact with the Devil actually *was* a pact. One such has survived the years, by some odd chance, for a pact normally was supposed to disappear with the spirit to whom it was given. But the pact made by Urbain Grandier, a priest of Loudon in the seventeenth century, was somehow preserved. It read in part: "I give you my body, my soul, and my life . . . Signed Urbain Grandier in his blood."

The practices of witches throughout Europe varied, of course, but their confessions showed that their habits were basically the same. Some of the accused were not witches. They were cranks, or persons hated by their neighbors who denounced them, but there were hundreds of men and women who earnestly renounced Christianity and sought to serve what they called the Devil.

How could one serve the Devil? How did one become a witch? Often it was simple: Where witchcraft was strong children would be dedicated from birth, or from puberty, either by baptism or confirmation. The witches, as well as the Church, had their midwives. The midwives licensed by the Church, usually men, hastened to baptize infants after birth if no priest were present, before the witches had time to cast their evil spells. But the witch midwives were also alert to dedicate the babies to Satan as they were born.

However, if a person wished to become a witch, and was not committed at birth, the path was relatively easy. Either one of the local cult recognized that a person was susceptible to witchcraft, and was thus approached about joining the coven, or one could seek out a witch friend and apply. Sometimes, however, there were those who were not eager to become witches, but after pressure, promises and threats were persuaded to join the local sect. The fear of what the demons, who were everywhere, would do (for example, twist necks, burn houses) was often enough to persuade the uncertain to become witches.

The first step in becoming a witch was for the prospective servant of the Devil to assert that this was a free and willing desire (an assertion that was sometimes the result of pressure). Second was the denial of the Christian faith, and third the signing of a pact with the Devil. This pact could be verbal or written, but it was a vow to the Devil, as represented by the master of the local coven. Then the witch generally was formally introduced to the coven. The coven was the inner circle of practicing witches in an area. (The word coven seems to be a derivative of "covene.") The initiation into witchhood could be done privately, or in the coven, or even at a larger meeting, the Sabbat.

In the coven the new witch renounced Christianity (perhaps spitting on the cross) and gave his or her vows to the Devil. The master of the ceremonies, or chief Devil, would place one hand on the crown of the head of the witch candidate and the other on the sole of the foot and declare that henceforth all that was between his hands —body and soul—were in the Devil's service. (Some reports indicate that the witches placed the hands and made the dedications.)

After this, there generally followed a ceremony of baptism with the witch being given a Devil-name. This secret name might have been given in the hope of escaping the good spirits' watchfulness. Some recorded names were "Thief of Heaven," "Pickle-Nearest-the-Wind," and "Batter-Them-Down Maggy" (the latter two in Scotland).

If the pact was written, the witches signed in blood. Sometime during the initiation, the skin of the candidate was cut so that he bled. Most witches could not read or write, but they could make their mark. After the witch had pledged to serve the Devil, his or her name was entered in the Black Book or Roll, which was kept by the master of the coven. The witch was admonished to keep witch affairs secret; secrecy was most important to witchcraft. In one case the coven's chief did not trust a witch awaiting trial in prison and his emissaries went into the prison and hanged the witch before he had any chance to repeat "witches' tales."

After the witch made the vows, he received a mark from the Devil. This mark, when discovered by those trying to rout out witchcraft, was considered a sure sign of guilt, especially when pricked without bleeding or causing pain. (The importance of this mark in showing guilt proved to be unfortunate for many innocent persons who were condemned only on the basis of having some unusual spot or natural mark, which was mistaken for a witch mark.)

The witches were given a mark as part of their initiation by being either scratched or bitten by the master Devil of the coven. Some substance was then rubbed into the wound, leaving a permanent mark like a tattoo. Sometimes this mark was red, sometimes blue. Some marks, described in trials, were small and circular like fleabites. Others were in the shapes of various animals, perhaps a dog, a toad, a bat or a mouse. Sometimes the mark was made on a prominent place, such as on the shoulder, or it might be concealed, such as under the eyelids or lips.

Some say that a drug was given to the witches at the time of their initiation. The drug, plus the excitement and hysteria, made the initiation a truly impressive ceremony.

The newly initiated witch became a formal member of the local coven, which generally consisted of thirteen members: twelve ordinary witches—men and women—and the master, or Devil, usually a man. Of course, there were the odd witches who did not belong to any such formalized group, but generally the witchcraft of an area was in the hands of the coven. These members held a weekly meeting, an *esbat*, at which various nefarious witch business was discussed. This meeting was held at any convenient place, which was kept secret from the outside world. The witches would report their doings since the last meeting, receive orders and learn about new poisons or interesting processes for doing the Devil's work.

As they sat or knelt in a circle, the chief of the coven would pass around the poison. The witches squatting with their knees drawn up to the chins and hands clasped before them, would rock back and forth. Chanting and chanting, they rocked, mumbling such words as "Shurius, Turius, Tirus." They would receive the poison (which had been properly cursed) in their outstretched hands. The witch's skill at poisoning was universally feared. Henry VIII had such respect for the witches' ability that he authorized that all poisoners should, upon conviction, be boiled to death. By the Middle Ages, witches were accused of such activities as poisoning wells and widely distributing toadstools.

Wax candles were used at the meetings. According to tradition these were made by witches in the moonlight, and were composed of hair from a hanged man, fat from the cauldron into which dozens of noxious items had been thrown, together with the finger of a murderer whose grave had been robbed. Supposedly if one of these candles was held to a lock, the spring would fly back and the most heavily locked door would open.

The *esbat* was a rather modest, practical meeting. There might well be cakes, meat, beer and other drink, and surely there would be music of some kind, and dancing. The Grand Master, or Devil, was the executive at these ordinary meetings. Generally speaking he went to these sessions and about his own daily business in normal dress. However, there did seem to be a pattern to his appearance: sombre clothes, a tall hat and garters. (Garters are still given mystical qualities, such as being a means of bewitching cattle or defending against a spell.) How the leader of the cult, the Devil, changed for the more grandiose meetings, called the Sabbats! He *became* the Devil, by disguise. Sometimes his identity was known to the witches, often it was not, for his appearance was so horrifying, his transformation so complete, that his name could not be found out.

The Devil for centuries had often been thought of as a huge black monster with horns on his head, cloven hoofs, ass's ears, hair, claws, fiery eyes and fierce teeth. The Devil of the medieval Sabbat could assume many shapes, but most assuredly he wore a mask, a horrifying mask perhaps with horns, and often in the form of an animal. The Devil's body was covered with skins, hair, paint, charms and ointments.

Throughout Europe the disguise of the Devil varied. The bull's form was common. In Lorraine, we learn, the Devil often appeared as a goat, sometimes with a candle between his horns. Sometimes in France the Devil was a goat. In the British Isles, the horse form was common. The Devil could also appear as cat, bear, stag, boar, dog or wolf. Whatever his disguise, he was the god, the Grand Master, the Grand Devil of the celebration.

The Sabbat (or Sabbath) was the festival of the various covens of a given district. This great meeting would be held in some secluded place, near a lake, or in the heart of a forest, in a meadow or a cave. Any spot that seemed to have mystical properties could be utilized. The Black Forest on the Hartz Mountains in Germany was long held as a meeting place of witches.

The dates of the festivals varied throughout Europe, but a general pattern was discernible. The spring festival came on the eve of May Day, April 30. In Germany this festival was called Walpurgisnacht, in England it was Roodmas. The second great festival was held on October 31. Others included Candlemas on February 2, Lammas on August 1, St. Thomas Day on December 21 and the Eve of St. John on June 23.

Children admitted to the Sabbat for the first time

For centuries the Sabbats were gossiped about as being fantastic, horrible, drunken, wild orgies. Perhaps they were some of that. But the witches — a group immersed in years of legend and mythology — did convene to protest against the orthodox religion, Christianity, that was imposed upon them. They were excited, stimulated worshippers of a cult they believed in. There are various viewpoints as to what is possibly believable about these Sabbats, and what could only be the results of frightened, tortured imaginations of those testifying under pressure at trials. But as the savage tribal festivals among primitive peoples of today are real, it is conceivable that the Sabbats did occur as described.

What happened at these witch gatherings? To understand the atmosphere of the Sabbat, one must first study how the witches were transported to these midnight-to-cockcrow sessions. The traditional picture is of the witches flying on broomsticks to the Sabbat. Most probably, however, most of the witches walked, only those more prosperous going on horseback. Nevertheless, a solid number of witches believed that they actually flew to the meetings. It is

Sorceries scene: witch riding through the air on the Devil; an enchanted castle; a fairy ring; a friar raising his imps; spirit raised by a witch

certain that they did anoint themselves with a flying ointment before setting out. This ointment consisted of grease and a number of vile properties that the witches considered noxious or obscene, such as certain herbs and drugs. A famous description of the ointment was given by Reginald Scott in his *Discoverie of Witchcraft* on 1584:

They seethe [the fat] with water in a brazen vessell, reserving the thickest of that which remaineth boiled at the bottom which they lay up and keep until occasion serveth to use it . . . They put hereunto Eleoselinum Aconitum, belladonna, soote and Solanum Somniferum. They mix all these together, and then they rub all parts of their bodies exceedingly till they look red and be very hot, so as the pores may be opened and their flesh soluble and loose. They join herewithal either fat or oil that the force of the ointment may pierce inwards and so be more effectual. . . .

A later historian, A. J. Clark, analyzed some of the recipes for flying magic and found that some listed ingredients would indeed be drugs that could produce mental confusion, dizziness, excitement and irregular heart action. No wonder the witches felt that they were flying!

Preserved is Isobel Gowdie's flying charm, to which she confessed at her trial as a witch:

I had a little horse and would say "Horse and Hattock in the Devil's name." And then we would fly where we would, even as straws would fly upon a highway. We fly like straws when we please; wild straws and corn-straws will be horses to us, and we put them betwixt our feet and say "Horse and Hattock in the Devil's name."

After the witches had convened, the first process was a roll call. New witches would be introduced. All would make their reports on the deviltry they had accomplished and make vows to continue the dedication of their souls to the Devil. Perhaps the witches would be asked to kiss the Devil as he existed at the Sabbat in his horrible disguise. Then the dancing began. This could be ordinary folk dancing with clothes on, or a wilder type with the witches naked except for masks. There was music, played on the instruments of the day, perhaps the violin or pipes or tambourine.

Always a number of routine dances were included in the festivities. Ring dances were held around a central object, whether it was the Devil, a tree or a stone. The follow-the-leader dance always had an end man who whipped those lagging behind. Dances were performed sitting on branches or upon broomsticks, and there was much leaping and cavorting. Food would be served, and it would vary according to the status of those who provided it. According to witch testimonies the bread could be "like wafers, the drink was sometimes blood, and other times black moss-water." Or perhaps "beefe, bacon and roasted mutton" were served. Whatever it was, it is sure that there was much eating and drinking and an atmosphere of frenzied enjoyment, with the participants buoyed by the drugs and wine, until cockcrow called a halt to the festivities. It is easy to understand why Christians considered the witches' Sabbats demoniac exhibitions.

Even though participation in the Sabbat was considered anti-Church, and thus contrary to society's rules, most witches were tried and condemned for individual acts of witchcraft. And to be crimes, such acts had to be shown to be malevolent, done at the bidding of an evil power— the Devil. White magic, such as healing or causing crops to prosper, was not considered witchcraft, nor was astrology, which was used by rulers throughout Europe for centuries.

What *was* witchcraft was a black deed, such as putting pins in images to cause death, or concocting a poison to kill —these were done with evil intent with the aid of evil force.

The witch had many individual skills that were feared and punished. One was said to be the ability to change shape—to become, under certain circumstances, a bird, a fish, a reptile or other animal. Many primitive peoples believed this to be possible and natural—a change brought about by devils, or by magic, or as the result of a curse.

In early days in northern Europe it was thought that a man could become a wolf or a bear by wearing the skins of those animals, or by rubbing a magical salve on his body. If one rolled naked on the ground under a new moon one might become a werewolf. Sometimes witches could change shapes by speaking charms. In medieval days the Church denied that any such transformation could occur, and said

Possessed man begging his family not to denounce him to the magistrates

that those who claimed they changed shapes had minds clouded by delusions of demons, which made them *think* they had been transformed. If a man thought, for example, that he had run about as a cat or a wolf, he was deluded and would be punished only for his imaginings, and not for his actions. However, as the hysteria about witches grew through the years, this shape-changing became identified with witchcraft, and by the fourteenth century was. punished, often by death.

As late as the early nineteenth century witches were supposed to run about in animal shapes and suffer in their own selves whatever happened to them in the animal shape. Isobel Gowdie at her trial as a witch confessed thus:

"When we go in the shape of a hare, we say thrice over:

> *I shall go intill a hare,*
> *With sorrow and sych and meikle care;*
> *And I shall go in the Devil's name*
> *Ay while I come home again.*

"An instant we start in a hare. And when we would be out of that shape, we will say,

> *Hare, hare, God send thee care.*
> *I am in a hare's likeness just now*
> *But I shall be in a woman's likeness even now.*

Isobel Gowdie said that the Devil would often send her on errands as a hare, and concluded that "The dogs will sometimes get some bites of us, when we are in hares, but will not get us killed."

Thus, in shape-changing, the witch *became* the animal for a time. In the trial of Bartie Paterson, in 1607, it was

A witch and her imps, A.D. 1621 (from contemporary drawing)

testified that the accused was a witch because she had disguised herself as a cat and had, with other cats—that is to say, witches—given a serenade on a certain night in the backyard of one of the witnesses appearing at the trial. The evidence was believed and Bartie was hanged.

In barbaric days, it was thought that men could be transformed into wolves. So prevalent was the idea in many parts of the world where there were many wolves, that people were forbidden to speak of them, "Lest the wolves should hear and rend you."

Each region had its favorite animal. In India, it was thought that witches changed into tigers and leopards; in Africa, into lions and hyenas; in Iceland, into bears; and in England, the most popular shape was the cat.

It was also believed that every witch had a familiar spirit, and sometimes more than one. Demons were supposed to be able to manifest themselves in animal form. These animals were a sort of personal devil, who would obey all orders of the witch, with powers bestowed by Satan himself. Most of the animals were domestic creatures, minor demons who took the form of a cat or of a dog, toad, insect or other small creature, that lived with the witches. In return for doing the witch's work the animals were rewarded by drops of blood, sucked from pricked fingers, or from swellings on the witches. One Essex witch was supposed to have imps in the shape of a kitten, a rabbit, a polecat and a long-legged greyhound with a head like an ox.

Many witches testified at their trials that they had used familiars to cast spells. One said that she sent her little dog to afflict a man. Another said that it was through her cat that she was able to lame her husband. Still another said that she had sent her gray cat to torment a wife. Whatever the animal—and some witches claimed to use ferrets, rats, butterflies and wasps as their familiars—it is obvious that these animals were merely pets of lonely, imaginative people.

Many witches also boasted of having "the evil eye," by which they were able to bewitch or even kill by a glance. In more than one trial witches confessed that Satan had told them, "If you bear ill-will to anybody, look on them with open eyes, and pray evil for them in my name and you will get your heart's desires."

The belief in the evil eye was widespread; even officials of the early Church believed in it. The people took the power of the evil eye seriously, and believed that if they were bewitched by it, only immediate countermeasures would save them. By raising one's hands to one's eye, the power of the evil glance could be averted. So often was this gesture made that a charm representing the hand came into existence. Horseshoes nailed over a door were supposed to protect from witchcraft in general, but from the evil eye in particular.

The ability to murder or cripple or harm in some way through the use of image magic has long been attributed to witches. Certainly image magic was practiced in ancient Babylon and India, in Egypt, classical Greece and Rome, and flourished for centuries after the coming of Christianity. The theory was that whatever was done to the image would in truth happen to the original of the image. The image had a magical identification with the victim, and was thus for all practical witchcraft purposes the same as the man or woman for whom murder or harm was intended.

A figure roughly resembling the victim was made of wax, clay, wood or metal, and baptized in his name. Sometimes an existing portrait was used instead of an image; almost anything could be symbolically used if the proper rites were performed over it. Sometimes a living

The witch of Endor evoking the Prophet Samuel (Johann Heinrich Schönfeld; seventeenth century)

Witch raising a storm

animal, a bird or a toad, for example, was tortured and killed in the belief that the human being would suffer and die with it. In the manufactured images, something belonging to the victim was generally incorporated, so that the identification would be stronger. Perhaps a piece of hair, nail parings or shreds of clothing were added. The image was stabbed with pins, thorns or nails, and either melted slowly before a fire or left to decay in earth or running water. As this happened the victim was supposed to feel great pain, waste away mysteriously as the image melted or decayed, or die suddenly when the heart was pierced. The victim could be saved only if the charmed thing was discovered and immediately destroyed.

Spells often were used with the image magic. The victim was to come under the spell, and the spell was supposed to kill by the ninth day. If it did not, then the witch used poison.

Sorcerer selling mariners the winds tied up in three knots of a rope

Sometimes just a spell was supposed to cause death or injury. Curses were often inscribed on tablets and put in graves or in some secret places, and as long as the tablets lay undiscovered, misfortune would continue to fall on the victims.

Witches have long been credited with being able to control natural phenomena, bring storms at sea, cause rain and drought and summon fogs, hail, frost, snow and thunder. They were considered especially adept at controlling the wind. They would even sell the wind, which was tied in knots upon a thread, to sailors. When they needed stronger wind they loosened a knot. In the sixteenth century the North Berwick witches confessed that they had caused a violent storm by throwing a cat into the sea. In the same century another witch was said to have drowned a dozen sailors by moving eggs about in a pail of water, as part of a magic rite. In a Scottish trial it was learned that the witches controlled the elements thus:

> . . . *an old doting woman casteth a flint stone over her left shoulder towards the west, or hurleth a little sea-sand up into the element, or wetteth a broom-sprig, and sprinkleth the same into the air, or diggeth a pit in the earth, and putting water therein, stirreth it about with her finger or boileth hog's bristles or layeth sticks across upon a bank where never a drop of water is or buryeth sage till it be rotten, all which things are confessed by witches, and affirmed by writers to be the means that witches use to move extraordinary tempests and rain.*

In Scotland, witches wishing to shipwreck a vessel put a milk pan full of water on the floor, and floated a small round dish in it. Then they began their incantations. When the dish upset, the ship was supposed to sink.

Thus witches controlled events, according to all those who believed in them. They could kill, they could harm, they could destroy. That they were evil had been accepted for centuries. That they owed allegiance to the Devil was also accepted. From a pre-Christian, semitolerant attitude toward witches, sentiment changed. The Church became more powerful each year until it was in a position to stamp out hundreds and hundreds of lives, in the belief it was routing out those who challenged it and God.

Part II
Persecution of
Witches

In the early days of Greece and Rome, witchcraft did
not flourish as a cult. There was no highly organized group
that could be persecuted. As a result of centuries of worship
of various gods and goddesses there were many different
religions and great religious tolerance. It did not matter
so much to which god one owed allegiance, but rather
which temporal ruler one revered and obeyed. Early cases
of witching, whether by astrology or fortune-telling or
chanting, were thus looked upon with favor or disfavor

according to the ideas of the secular ruler of the time.

Sorcery was considered evil when it threatened or disturbed those who governed. That is why, for example, the official, Hui, in Egypt was forced to commit suicide in 1200 B.C.—for he had, with his wax image magic, threatened the power of the ruler, Rameses III. And yet, as we have seen, even the rulers utilized the priest-sorcerers and astrologers.

In ancient Greece, Aristotle was said to have played the role of wizard in instructing Alexander the Great. He gave Alexander a number of wax figures nailed down in a box fastened by a chain, which he was to carry with him at all times. Each time he lifted the box up or set it down he was to make certain incantations. These wax figures were images of Alexander's potential enemies. These wax armed men held swords pointing backward, others had spears that had no heads, others had cut strings to their bows. All these figures were placed downward in the box. Aristotle believed that Alexander, with such a box of impotent enemies, would be safe from attack in real life. This was witchcraft in early Greece. Yet, during the same period, Theoris, a Greek woman, was tried publicly in Athens and burned for her sorceries.

Spells for evil purposes were punished by death according to the laws of the fifth century B.C. In 139 B.C. an edict ordered all astrologers to leave Rome, but they came flocking back after that, because the public wanted them and used them. The astrologers even began composing almanacs and books. Literature and legends told of the werewolves and witches and supernatural fantasies. Virgil, whose works were among the most famous of Latin literature, was regarded as skilled in occultism. Pliny's writing contained magic recipes. For example, he said, to cure gout, "rub the limb with oil, in which have been distilled the intestines of frogs and a dead toad burned to ashes." If you have a fever, "wear as an amulet the carcass of a frog minus the claws and wrapped in a piece of russet-coloured cloth."

The Roman emperors continued to dabble in black magic. Those who punished magic often did so because they feared it would be used in conspiracies against their power. With the coming of Christianity, there was an effort to wipe out the old beliefs and worships of the pagans. But in 313 A.D., the Edict of Milan seemed to insure that all religions would be equally tolerated by the governments. Then, less than a decade later, laws were passed against astrology and magic as practiced by those who had not accepted the new religion of Christianity. Constantius, in 353, had a law passed which forbade sacrifices at night. Four years later he passed more encompassing laws: "There shall be no more divination nor curious inquiries, nevermore. Whosoever shall dare disobey this statute shall lose his head by the avenging sword of the executioner." The various types of magicians were named: "Let no man consult any astrologer, fortune-tellers, augurs, seers, and the whole dark fraternity shall exercise their arts no more."

There followed a period in which pagan temples were reopened and astrologers and magicians were warmly welcomed by the emperors again. Then, in 367, an incident occurred that brought forth the full wrath of the emperor against the magic-makers and set off a hysterical purge of all those suspected of sorcery.

Valens was on the throne. One of his high officials, Theodorus, sought to discover who would succeed Valens. Two highly regarded astrologers were called in and there took place a type of spirit rapping in which the spirit supposedly rapped out a name considerably similar to Theodorus. Valens heard of this and became furious, and determined once and for all to wipe out all occultists and magicians. All those involved in this incident were killed, but the campaign did not stop there. Anyone and everyone became suspect, and many innocent persons lost their lives.

One old woman was put to death because it was common knowledge that she could cure fevers by chanting certain magic rhymes. Houses of wealthy merchants were searched for incriminating magical documents. People destroyed their books and other possessions for fear of being considered magic-makers. Panic was everywhere and no one trusted anyone else as Valens carried out his purge.

The laws remained stringent through the reigns of the following emperors. An edict in 381 prohibited any night sacrifices, or any meetings at all at night in old temples. Honorious, in 399, reiterated penalties against those who offered "unhallowed sacrifices," and pagan altars were ordered destroyed.

Yet even in the Roman Empire there were no general anti-witchcraft laws. Often the control of witchcraft was placed in the hands of the local authorities. Through the early years of the Christian era, in some periods there was strict adherence to anti-magic laws, in others there was a greater tolerance. The laws and punishments varied throughout the whole of Europe, but as governments and Christianity slowly became more stable, paganism and the rites that had long been associated with it became less tolerated. Year by year witchcraft became more closely associated with heresy in the eyes of the Church.

In church rules issued in England by St. Theodore, seventh Archbishop of Canterbury, one whole section was devoted to magic practices and ceremonies, with penance assigned to each misdoing. For example, "If anyone sacrifies to demons, one year of penance if he be a clown of low estate, if he be of high degree, 10 years."

There was evidence that in England, as well as on the continent, witchcraft and sorcery were widely practiced. It was said that storms were raised, cattle were killed and enemies were afflicted with disease, but the punishment for witchcraft was not as harsh as that inflicted by the early Roman emperors.

In a document of the Archbishop of York in the eighth century, penances are listed: "If any woman practise any magic arts, or spells, and work evil charms, let her fast for a twelvemonth. . . . If she has slain any one by her evil charms, let her fast for VII years." In the same century the Council of Cloves directed its bishops to go out to their dioceses annually, "to teach the word of God," and forbade pagan activities, which were defined as "soothsayers, sorcerers, auguries, auspices, amulets, spells, or all the filth of the impious and errors of the heathen."

By the tenth century in England the laws of Edward and Gunthrun provided that if witches, perjurers or diviners be found anywhere "let them be driven from the country . . . or let them totally perish within the country, unless they desist." Excommunication from the church was also to be enforced if the magician did not reform. Trying to change the course of love also was legislated against. Any cleric or layman who, to gain love, practiced any witchcraft in food or drink or by spells would be forced to do penance. Magic—both black and white—was considered pagan and devilish in early England and therefore punishable by penance.

Scotland, even in its very early history, had legends of witchcraft. In the second century a king was said to have learned through witchcraft of a conspiracy against him. It was reported in the fourth century that a group of witches in Scotland gathered together to try to kill St. Patrick. As he was sailing on the sea the witches, by chanting, threw

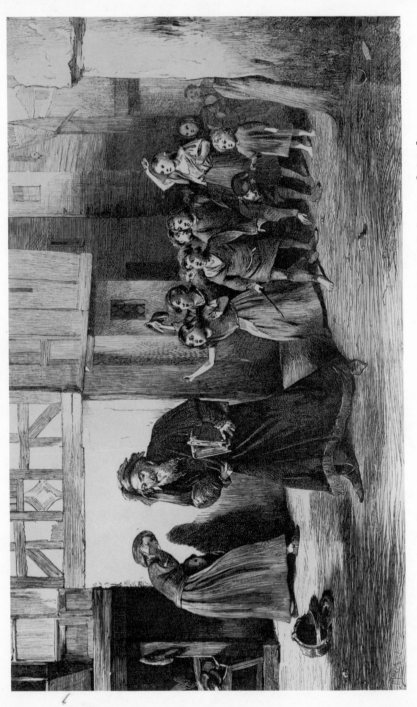

"Adam Warner Hooted as a Wizard" (by H.B. Roberts; from exhibition of the Royal Academy)

a huge rock at his vessel. The rock, which did not hit its mark, became in later days the fortress of Dumbarton. Of course, St. Patrick was unharmed. By the ninth century King Kenneth I had ordered that all those who invoke spirits "and use to seek upon them for helpe, let them be burnt to death." And in the tenth century when a gang of witches who had made a wax image of King Duffus were caught roasting it on a long spit over a slow fire, they were burned to death.

In France, as early as the fifth century, laws were passed against the practice of witchcraft. Here, too, however, punishments were not severe. The Salic Law listed fines for a curse, or a witch's knot, or for accusing anyone of having assisted at a Sabbat. This was government law; Church law was also leveled against the witch. If the witch was of high rank, he or she was to be publicly excommunicated. If the witch was of lower rank, or a slave, he was to be beaten so that he would learn his lesson.

Bishops in the sixth century ordered witches denounced and, after being punished, sold as slaves. Throughout the first dynasty of French kings there continued to be legislation against witches; the punishment was chiefly heavy fines. Occasionally there were cases in which the death penalty was invoked, but these generally involved persons in high office, and it is most likely that such persecution was on a political basis rather than simple opposition to witchcraft.

Under Charlemagne more laws were passed against chanters, wizards and other doers of magic, but here again the penalties were relatively light, with imprisonment and a season for repentance. However, by the time of the rule of Charlemagne's son, King Louis, the Church was becoming greatly concerned by what it considered the growth of sorcery. The church officials appealed to Louis to help them stamp out witchcraft. They repeated the contention that there was much in the Bible that ordained that witches should be severely punished. As in other countries, and in other times, these church officials specifically pointed out Exodus, xxii: 18, which stated, "Wizards thou shalt not suffer to live." They urged that witches, whether men or women, "must be sharply and cogently punished by the Prince of the land, seeing that they have arrived at such a point of wickedness as to transfer their allegiance to Satan."

Thus, in France, witchcraft was now identified with heresy. So in the time of Charles the Bald, in 873, a rule was set forth: "It is the duty of Kings to slay the wicked, not to suffer witches and poisoners to live . . . all and any such shall be sought out and taken. If they be found guilty, whether men or whether women, let them die the death as law and justice demand." This law was to be far-reaching for it did not condemn just the practicing witches but "also those who consort with or consult them."

There were some cases in which the accused denied their guilt; then, if the evidence against them was not conclusive, a test called a "Judgment of God" was made. The most popular of these tests for proving or disproving witchcraft was the ordeal by water. Ordeals had been used for years for various crimes, but now the ordeal by water seemed especially suitable for determining whether a person was a witch.

The accused was tied thumbs to toes, and sometimes with a rope around the middle, and put down into water that had been blessed by a priest. The water could be a reservoir, a pool or a running stream. If the suspect sank, the charge of witchcraft was considered false. If he did not sink that was proof beyond all doubt that the accused *was* a witch.

Other ordeals were often used to determine guilt. The hot-iron ordeal consisted of forcing the suspect to pick up a red-hot bar of metal, which he had to hold for a few moments. Then the hand was wrapped in bandages, which were sealed. On the third day the bandages were removed, and if there was no trace of burning the accused was innocent. The same idea was used in the ordeal of boiling water. Then the suspect's arm was plunged into a steaming cauldron and some object, such as a ring, was recovered from the bottom of the cauldron. If in three days the arm of the accused showed no sign of scalding, then he was not guilty.

However, there were relatively few witch trials compared to those that would follow in France, or, for that matter, in all of Europe, during the twelfth and thirteenth centuries. Christianity came slowly to Germany, and as a result there were many groups that did not adhere to official Christian doctrine by this time, and as elsewhere, these were identified with witchcraft. So much so, that most witch cases were tried by the papal inquisitors rather than the civil courts. Some witches were hanged, others were imprisoned and often dragged out of their jails by the townspeople and burned alive.

Various groups fought the church and temporal powers. There were Satanists who "devoted themselves to the most monstrous profanations, and stopped at nothing to spread their devilish doctrines." There were the Stedingers, thirteenth-century peasants who resisted Christianity and adhered to certain pagan practices and superstitions. They revolted against the rule of the archbishop, then embarked on a campaign of death and destruction. They burned churches and monasteries, killed many at will. They were accused, in addition to their rebellious crimes, of sorcery and were excommunicated. This action merely raised the fury of the Stedingers. Finally a crusade against them was called for by the Pope who ordered that the abominable witches and wizards be rooted out. He said they were "seduced by the Devil, abjured all laws of God and man, slandered the Church . . . consulted witches to raise evil spirits, shed blood like water, taken the lives of priests and concocted an infernal scheme to propagate the worship of the Devil. . . . The Devil appears to them in different shapes—sometimes as a goose or a duck, and at others in the figure of a pale black-eyed youth, with a melancholy aspect. . . . This Devil presides at their Sabbats, when they all kiss him and dance around him."

Bishops, dukes, counts and other nobles finally assembled an army of 40,000 men who marched against the Stedingers. The heretics were defeated and 8,000 of their dead were left on the field. That was the end of their revolt which, of course, was not really opposed because individuals were practicing magic, but because a dissident group threatened the very existence of both church and secular power.

In the centuries to come, throughout all Europe more and more individuals would be accused and tried and punished by death for their singular magical abilities. This came about largely through the Inquisition, which was initially established to rout out those who were merely anti-Church. In the late twelfth century, popes and emperors had decreed that heresy should be punished by death. Innocent III hastened the process of witch-hunting by sending letters to the secular princes demanding action against heretics.

Pope Gregory IX in 1233 wrote the bishops in southern France that he intended to employ preaching friars for the discovery and repression of heresy. Thereby, the Inquisition was truly established. At first, the emissaries of the Pope

traveled from district to district. They called upon the
people to confess their heresy or to denounce those they
knew to be heretics. A month's time was given and those
who confessed were punished lightly. Then came the Inquisition for those who had not confessed. It continued
until the district was declared to be free of those against
the church. Later, in every parish the priest and several
laymen were empowered to search out those who believed
in false doctrines and bring them to trial and punishment.
The monasteries then took over from the priests. The kings
of France even gave subsidies to the inquisitors, whose
powers were absolute.

In the Inquisition, the accused was surprised by a
sudden summons, was presumed guilty and was not informed about the witnesses against him. Women, children
and slaves could be witnesses for the prosecution, but not
for the defense. Informers were encouraged. Those who
confessed and denounced other heretics were "reconciled"
with the church, were punished only by penances, fasting,
prayers and pilgrimages and were made to wear on their
breasts or backs, crosses of yellow felt sewn onto the clothes.
Those who refused to confess were subject to physical
torture. If they still maintained their innocence they were
turned over to the civil government for punishment—which
meant death.

Since witchcraft was now so closely allied with heresy,
hundreds of so-called witches were killed in the years after
the setting up of the Inquisition. All through the fourteenth
century the trials went on in Europe. The Church fought
against new ideas and the old religions. There arose a frenzy
that heretics must die and witches must burn. The trials
and burnings mounted into the thousands. The ordinary
people suffered under the fury.

In France, eleven witches were turned over to the civil

government for execution. Three of the eleven were shepherds who were convicted of having killed cattle and flocks of sheep by evil spells; eight women had concocted philtres, fashioned amulets and openly practiced divination. One confessed she had frequently attended the Sabbats. Those arrested as heretics were examined for their powers in witchcraft. At Toulouse a solemn public burning was held in which sixty-three people were consumed by the flames. Two shepherds were found guilty of having poisoned various wells and also of having sacrificed a black cock one midnight in order to bring war upon another district. They were burned alive.

In Carcassonne, France, in a period of thirty years in the first half of the fourteenth century, the Inquisition heard 400 cases and burned 200 persons who had been accused as witches. In Toulouse during the same period the Inquisition heard 600 cases and sent 400 witches to the stake.

Hundreds of innocent persons were burned, of course. But among the accused there were always some who freely confessed their black crimes. Anne-Marie de Georgel and Catherine Delort said that they attended the Sabbats and that they adored the Demon who was there in the form of a large black goat. They said they offered stolen infants to the Grand Master, that the Devil was equal to God, that the Devil ruled on earth and God in heaven. Obviously they *did* belong to a heretical sect and undoubtedly did go to nightly meetings where evildoing was practiced.

By the beginning of the fifteenth century the war against heretics and witches had intensified, and cases began appearing even among those high in society. In 1419, King Henry V of England publicly revealed that his stepmother, Joan of Navarre, had, by means of magic and evil arts, made attempts on his life. Joan of Arc was accused of demon-worship at trees and fountains, among other crimes. The Duchess of Gloucester, wife of the Regent of England, was found guilty of magical practices. One of the most horrible and flagrant cases of witchcraft involved Gilles de Rais, one of the greatest lords of France, who was put to death for Devil worship and the killing and sacrifice of children. There was more and more talk of the Devil, more suspicion, more trials and more torture. Death by burning was always the penalty.

Torture was applied even before the victim was burned. In 1462 eight men and women were tried for witchcraft. At first they denied their crimes; then they were tortured and they confessed. They were sentenced to be burned and one of the women, who had been accused of eating children, was made to sit naked for three minutes on red-hot iron before being burned. A man named Jean Grehaudi, accused of having "trampled on our Lord in the Sacrament" was made to go naked to the execution site. There, one of his feet was cut off and he was forced to kiss the sign of the cross on the ground. Then he was burned.

The work of stamping out witchcraft became more severe after the publication of a horrifying book, at the end of the fifteenth century, by James Sprenger, a Dominican novice. Sprenger had become the provincial, or chief prosecutor, of the German provinces about 1480 and was made General Inquisitor for Germany. He and another devout Dominican, Father Henry Kramer, wrote a book entitled *Malleus Maleficarum* which, backed by a papal bull, became for centuries the guidebook for the Catholic attack on sorcery.

The authors were undoubtedly sincere in their belief that a great effort was being made by the Devil to eradicate faith in God. They feared the Devil, who lured men and women to follow him as witches. Their book was a study of principles, a discussion of the nature of the Devil and witches; but most important of all, it described in detail the practical ways witches could be caught and burned. The authors believed malice was threatening the Church everywhere. Evil must be stamped out, they said—the authorities must attack to save the Church.

But how could the courts find the thousands of people who were instruments of the Devil? Everyone knew, the *Malleus* said, that the mother who was a witch took her child and raised it up and presented it to the "other God." Yes, the church knew that the witch-midwife desired either to kill the newborn child or offer it to the Devil. The main thing was to keep these children from being baptized.

In addition to the midwives who were suspected of being witches, there were great lords who used unlawful enchanters, and wise women in the villages. Witches were everywhere, according to the authors of the *Malleus.* Even apparent devotion to the Church did not make one immune from suspicion, for did not some of the witches make a show of faith?

The authors of the *Malleus* wrote out the blueprints for finding any and every one who might be a witch. The courts were to handle the cases. Whenever a judge—whether church or civil—came to an area, he posted a general summons on the public buildings, calling on everyone to tell him any suspicions or beliefs they might have about possible witches in the area. No one was to be punished if the accusations did not hold water. And everyone was welcome to tattle: criminals, excommunicated persons, convicted perjurers, children—all were encouraged to inform, to dig out the Devil's servants.

The informer informed, then the order was given for the arrest of the accused. The house was searched for instruments or signs of witchcraft. Any friends or servants in the house were seized. When the witch was arrested, it was considered advisable to put her in a basket or on a plank when she was carried away so she could not touch the ground. This way, not being in touch with the earth (the Devil's preserve), the witch would lose her power.

The accused was presumed to be guilty. She was not asked *whether* she committed a certain act, but *why* she did. If the witch confessed, she might be released if it was minor magic-making and did not concern harm to children or animals.

In most cases the accused was placed in prison. But the rules called for the witch to "freely confess" before being condemned to death; therefore, torture was necessary to compel the witch to confess so that she could be put to death. After torture, the witch might confess. But then she had to confess again without torture.

The witch was supposed to weep; often she could not, on command, so saliva was rubbed on her face to give the appearance of tears. She was shaved of all her hair. She had been searched for any signs of witchery, perhaps a bit of powder, or ash from the burned body of a child. If all failed, she was taken away and honest persons tried to persuade her to confess. She may even have been promised mercy, but that was always a false promise, for "mercy" would mean life imprisonment, or it might mean that the judge who promised it would then turn her over to another, who would sentence her to death.

One thing the witches could not demand was the ordeal by hot iron, for the judges knew that witches could, by the use of magic herbs, make themselves insensible to burning.

The torture was inhuman—the whip, fire, the rack, the thumbscrew, a studded chair slowly heated. No wonder thousands of innocent people confessed. One man confessed after the thumbscrews had been put on him "so that

Possessed during a Protestant sermon

the blood ran out at the nails." The torturers stripped him, tied his hands behind his back, and by means of rope and pulley, drew him up and let him fall eight times. He could endure no more and he confessed. His statements, he wrote his daughter, were "sheer lies and made-up things," but the thought of more torture was more than he could face.

The *Malleus* helped the judges, and the number of trials increased as did the number of people burned, which grew to fantastic proportions.

Despite the Reformation in the sixteenth century, tolerance of belief did not come. Instead, Protestants were even more violent about heresy and witchcraft than the Catholics had been. Again, there was reliance on the old Biblical caution: "Thou shalt not suffer a witch to live." Luther said of witches, "I would burn them all." Calvin, too, advocated severe punishment. So the executions continued.

One witch-hunter in Fulda, Germany, Balthasas Ross, asserted that because of his activities over 700 people were put to death. In Berne, there were 900 executions in a period of ten years. In the Alps in Werdenfels, in one year, there were fifty executions. In districts around Trier, in six years, there were 360 executions. So-called witches were beheaded or strangled before being burned. In 1505, in the Tyrol, a woman was tortured eighteen times. Toward the end of that century, the wife of an innkeeper in Nordlingeen was said to have been put to the torture fifty-six times. At Bamberg, in central Germany, a special witch prison was built. By the early years of the seventeenth century, which brought even more horrors, more torture and more executions, Bamberg had become known for its suppression of witchcraft. In a period of less than twenty-five years, the authorities there executed over 900 persons. It has been estimated that in Germany there were more than 100,000 convictions between 1610 and 1660.

Children were not immune from the witch-hunting. Sometimes they were taken to watch the executions. It is recorded that at one such ceremony in northern Germany the clergy, the schoolchildren and the onlookers all sang hymns loudly. In Hungary a young boy bragged to a playmate that he could raise storms. At suppertime that evening there was a storm. The playmate told what he knew to his father, who told the authorities. Six men and seven women were burned as a result.

Children were taught to testify even against their parents. "Children of two," said one prosecutor, "can be interrogated in cases of witchcraft."

Informing lost its amateur status and became a professional occupation. The courts made great use of these traveling witchfinders.

By the sixteenth century, when Europe was aflame with burnings, England was considering laws against witches. Henry VIII, in 1541, had a statute enacted forbidding either the belief in or the practice of witchcraft. This statute was later repealed by Queen Elizabeth. But in 1562, the queen was urged on by two bishops who warned her that "the witches and sorcerers have increased marvellously." The result was a law providing that witches "suffer a year's imprisonment and be pilloried four times" for a first offense. For a second offense, the sentence was to be death by hanging. The crime was considered witchcraft only if "a person is wasted or injured by witchcraft." This was rather milder than what went on in the same period on the continent.

Hanging had been common in England since the beginning of the thirteenth century, when the populace had been urged to rout out thieves and other outlaws who,

Sorcerer being whipped by child

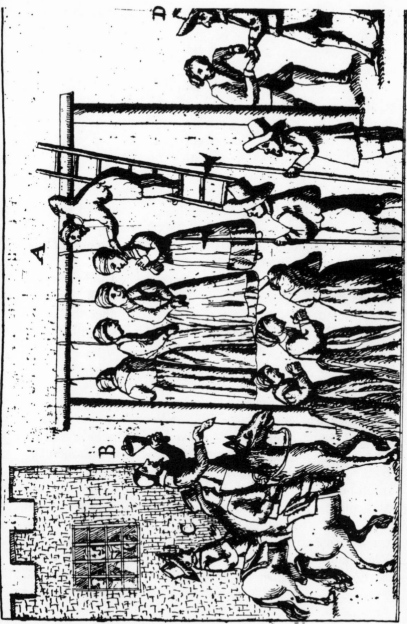

Execution of witches

after being caught, were hanged. The Tyburn Gallows, which stood near London, could accommodate as many as twenty-four victims at a time. It was a triangular arrangement of three uprights with beams across from corner to corner. When full, each beam could suspend as many as eight at one time. Among the many men and women who dangled from these gallows were witches. Sometimes the bodies, after they were removed, would be hanged again on a gibbet—an upright post with a projecting arm at the top—for display as a warning.

Though most witches were hanged, there were other punishments, too. In the thirteenth century an old woman and a young man accused of witchcraft were put between two walls of stone and plastered in alive. Sometimes the punishment was pressing. That is, the victim was placed on the floor, his arms and legs stretched out and fastened to iron rings so that his figure looked like an X. A sharp stone, about the size of a fist, was placed under the small of his back then, and a board or door loaded with heavy stones was placed on top of him.

Toward the end of the sixteenth century, a remarkable book appeared that urged stemming the wild tide of belief in witchcraft. For years, blame for bad crops, storms and pestilence had been placed on witches. Now there was a call to reason. Reginald Scott, an Oxford scholar, wrote *The Discoverie of Witchcraft*. Scot was a reformer; he pointed out that "childish absurdities" were at the root of all belief in witchcraft. He urged an end to the nonsense and called on the public and the government to be lenient with those accused out of spite or ignorance. The book caused concern among the intelligent. It also disturbed King James of Scotland, who was later to take the throne in England. He had all copies of the book burned, and proceeded to write his own ideas about witchcraft in *King James's Books Against Witchcraft and Daemonologie*.

Witches invoking rain

King James's book aroused even further those who wanted to believe in witchcraft. When he became King of England he saw to it that the law was far more severe than Elizabeth's had been. Witchcraft was now punishable by death on the first offense. Under the queen's law, death could be demanded only where an injury had been committed by use of witchcraft. Now, under King James, even believing in or consulting with evil spirits made a person liable to death. King James persecuted the witches because they were servants of the Devil, and as such would try to annihilate him, God's anointed. Enemies under the guise of witches would make attempts on his life. They were defying the king, they were treasonable, therefore they must be destroyed.

James I was bold in his persecution of witches. He went to one witch trial where a woman confessed that she had danced a reel before the Devil. He was so interested that he demanded a reenactment in the middle of the night. On another occasion, when he observed that one prisoner was stubborn about confessing his guilt as a witch, the king ordered the victim's fingernails to be pulled out with pincers, and two needles thrust in to their full length. When this did not make the accused confess, he was taken to the boote, a crushing instrument. There, he was abused until his legs were crushed together and the blood spouted out.

It was during the seventeenth century that a man named Matthew Hopkins reigned as informer in England. Hopkins was a thoroughly hateful man who spent his time "discovering witches" in the counties of Essex, Norfolk, Huntingdon and Suffolk. He was diabolical, a liar and a monster of cruelty. And he was paid for his efforts!

Hopkins was a lawyer of sorts and had been influenced by King James's book. In 1644 he was living at Manningtree, a small place in Essex County. With two assistants, he busied himself traveling about the countryside trying to ferret out witches. In each town he visited, he submitted a bill and was paid by the authorities for his work. He was quite effective in torturing his victims to make them confess. He had been empowered to examine all those suspected, for any reason at all, of witchcraft and then to extract a confession.

When Hopkins seized upon a person accused of witchcraft, the suspect was made to sit cross-legged on a stool or table in a barn. Then long pins were stuck in him, all over his body, in a search for the witch mark—the spot on his body that was insensitive to the pain of the pin-sticking. If any spot was found in which the victim did not cry out, that was the witch mark. Hopkins had a special instrument made. When it was pressed to the flesh, the pin retracted into the instrument, and did not stick the flesh. Then, of course, the accused did not feel any pain!

When the witch mark was discovered, the accused was

Water test for witchcraft

left with someone who waited for the Imp or Devil to show itself. Any ant or insect could be considered the Imp. One suspect was kept awake several nights by watchers who ran him forward and backward about the room until he collapsed of exhaustion, not caring what he said.

Hopkins also used the ordeal by water of "swimming the witch." He had the suspect, thumbs tied with string to his toes, taken to a pond. The accused was then placed in a sheet, the four corners of which were loosely tied together. Then the victim was put in the water and pulled across by a cord. If he floated, he was guilty. But if the "witch" sank and managed not to drown, proving his innocence, then the mob that was watching called for more tests. The accused might then be kept without food for three or four days, while forced to sit cross-legged.

Another test was the use of the scales and a great metal-bound Bible. A witch would be put on one side of a big pair of scales and weighed against the Bible. If the suspect weighed more than the Bible he went free, but if the Bible weighed more than the witch, it was the death sentence. This could be arranged, of course, with hidden weights and balances.

The people finally rose up against Hopkins, realizing that nobody would be safe from his witch-hunting. A cleryman in Huntingdonshire had the courage to write against the cruelties of witch-hunting in general and of Hopkins in particular. Opposition to Hopkins continued to grow, as did Hopkins' pay for finding witches. When Hopkins realized that public sentiment was turning against him, he published pamphlets to answer the questions raised about him. The pamphlets were signed:

By Matthew Hopkins

THE WITCHFINDER-GENERAL

FOR THE BENEFIT OF

THE WHOLE KINGDOM

1677

But public feeling against him had risen so that a few months after the publication of the pamphlets, it is said, the country people seized Hopkins and put *him* to the swimming test. Hopkins floated, therefore was guilty and was hanged as a wizard. And that was the end of the man who, in three years, had caused over 200 people to be killed.

The fury in England was spending itself. Inadequate evidence of witchcraft led many of the educated to turn away from the persecutions. The number of those brought to trial began to decline. A few hangings and lynchings were recorded in the late seventeenth century, but by 1736, the Act of George II had wiped out the severe anti-witchcraft laws. Penalties against those who practiced sorcery or fortune-telling, or otherwise dabbled in the occult, were again lightened. In England, men seemed to have regained their reason.

In Scotland, the trials and persecutions went on for a longer time. Back in the sixteenth century—in 1563—Queen Mary had an act passed that ruled that all witches and those who consulted with them would be punished by death. Thereafter, trial after trial was held in which the verdict was almost always the same: death by burning.

A woman in Fifeshire was convicted of practicing sorcery and was strangled and burned. The famous trial in 1591 against Gilly Duncan, Dr. Fian,. Agnes Sampson and other North Berwick witches resulted in executions. Dr. Fian, for example, was placed in a cart, strangled, then put into a great fire. This case was unusual in that the witches were involved in a political plot to overthrow King James. Perhaps because of this, under James the prosecution of witches in Scotland increased. Some were strangled, then burned. Some were thrust into a fire, pulled out and then thrown back in again.

One woman was haled before the courts for bewitching crops and corn. She went to the fire. Another confessed that she had cast a spell. She was burned. Another, a hideous hag, was accused of wrecking boats and drowning sailors, and making her neighbors pine and languish. "Justice" caught up with her. She was hanged and her body was burned. And so it went, from 1563 until James became King of England. More than 7,000 men, women and children had been executed. The last witch execution in Scotland took place in June, 1722. Two Highland women, a mother and daughter, were brought before the deputy sheriff and charged with witchcraft and consorting with the Devil. The mother was accused of having used her daughter as her "horse and haddock," causing her to be shod by the Devil. The daughter became lame in both her hands and her feet. The mother was sentenced to die and she went to the fire, first warming her hands over the flames that would consume her.

At long last, in 1736, the statutes in Scotland against witchcraft were repealed. The passions of persecution seemed to have been spent. The last official trial and execution for witchcraft in western Europe was in Switzerland in 1782. There, a woman named Anna Goeldi was accused by a doctor of having cast evil spells upon his young son, who was not well. Perhaps poison, that old witch's favorite, was involved. In any case, Anna Goeldi was hanged.

Less than a century before the witch-hunt ended by law in Scotland and England, the influence of the witchhunts of Matthew Hopkins was being felt in the Puritan colony of New England in America. The men and women who had emigrated to America brought with them the old beliefs in witchcraft. The outbreaks of trials and persecutions in the New World cannot be considered unusual. It is a wonder, in fact, that more trials and hangings did not take place.

In the history of witchcraft, the events in Massachusetts play only a small part. After all, in England during the seventeenth century there were hundreds of executions. In Scotland at least 3,400 people met their death as witches in the hundred-year period from 1580 to 1680. It has been estimated that in Europe millions died in the witch-hunts from the fourteenth to the seventeenth centuries. A more moderate estimate is half a million persons. In Alsace, on one occasion, 134 witches and wizards were burned. In the

Witchcraft at Salem Village

Basque country, in four months, over 600 were condemned to death. In the New World, from the first settlement to the end of the seventeenth century, only twenty-eight persons lost their lives in the Massachusetts witch-hunts. In the whole of New England the total was thirty-four.

Witchcraft in America has long been associated with the famous trials and hangings, in 1692, on Gallows Hill in Salem Village. This was the only large-scale witch-hunt in America and the nature of the outbreak was such that the antics of some excitable little girls brought hysteria to an entire village. The first suspicion of witchcraft came about 1645 in Springfield. There, several persons were said to be possessed, although no legal action was taken against the accused. In Connecticut, two years later, the first witch to be executed in New England was hanged. The next year a woman of Charlestown, maintaining her innocence to the last, was put to death.

In 1652, John Bradstreet was tried "for suspicion of having familiarity with the Devil. He said he read in a book of magic." Bradstreet was fined "20 shillings, or else to be whipped." In 1656 another woman was hanged; six years later, another. The public began to be aware that there was deviltry in the air. There were many cases of disturbances in which demons were said to have been active. One Nicholas Desborough was molested by stones, pieces of earth and cobs of Indian corn falling upon and about him. Sometimes these objects came in through the door, sometimes through a window or the chimney. In another household, doors were mysteriously shut and candlesticks thrown off the tables. In another, we are told, a frying pan hanging in the chimney rang so loud that not only those living in the house heard it, but also those who lived across the river. A general feeling of molestation by demons prevailed.

Cotton Mather

Two men helped fan the flames of hysteria in New England. They were father and son, Increase and Cotton Mather. Increase, who came from England to the New World, was a minister and active in community affairs. Cotton Mather, also a minister, was even more in the public eye. Both, by their writings and preachings (after all, Increase Mather had seen the recent witchcraft trials in England), kept the people aware of the danger of witchcraft and sorcery.

So the atmosphere was right for the outbreak of persecution in Salem Village in 1692. In February of that year a number of young children, fed by the tales of a West Indian slave, became hysterical. A doctor was called in and diagnosed the case. The children, he said, were under the influence of the Devil. From that point on, hysteria took over among the populace. The children provided name after name of those who were witches. As a result, by January, 1693, twenty persons were hanged and two died in prison. Many people feel that a good spanking given to the children could have averted the whole madness. Some authorities believe some type of witches' coven really existed in Salem Village. Because of the similarity of testimony by witnesses about the rites and rituals of the witches, it is thought by some that a secret witch society did exist. However, many innocent persons went to their death knowing and caring nothing about such activities.

In the light of what happened in Europe, it is remarkable that the witchcraft hysteria could be snuffed out so quickly once thoughtful men began to question it. The last execution for witchcraft in Massachusetts took place in 1692. There were no witch trials in New England after 1693. England and the rest of Europe, as has been noted, were slower in forsaking the witch madness. The last witch in Europe was burned a century later, in 1793, when the hag in Poland warmed her hands over the fire before she was burned.

Part III
Witches of
Note

A. ISOBEL GOWDIE

One of the most remarkable of all the world's witches was
Isobel Gowdie, a Scottish woman who had been practicing
her magic for over fifteen years before she made a voluntary
confession of her crimes. No one knew that Isobel Gowdie
was a witch, not even her husband, until she offered her
testimony in 1662.

She said she had been asked to join the cult some
years before, and did so by meeting the Devil in a parish
church one night. The first thing she was required to do

Asmodeus (witch devil)

was to deny her baptism. Then she put one of her hands to the crown of her head and the other to the sole of her foot and gave all that was between her two hands over to the Devil. He sat at a desk with a black book in his hands. She was brought forward by another witch for the Devil to baptize. According to the testimony at the trial, the Devil then marked her on the shoulder, sucked out some blood at the spot, spit it into his hand and then sprinkled it on her head saying, "I baptize thee, Janet, in my own name."

Thereafter, Isobel Gowdie met in the coven with the other witches. Isobel listed some of them, along with the "spirits" who waited upon them. Bessie Wilson was known as Throw the Corn Yard; another spirit was called The Roaring Lion; another, Thief of Hell. Witch Jean Marten was maiden of the coven, nicknamed Over the Dyke with It, because "the Devil always takes the Maiden in his hand next him, when we dance Gillatrypes and when we would leap . . . he and she will say 'Over the Dyke with It.'" Isobel and her sister witches were not just active at the coven meetings. There they planned their evil magic deeds, but they took themselves elsewhere to carry them out.

Isobel Gowdie joined several of the other witches: John Taylor and his wife, Janet Breadhead, Bessie Wilson and Margret Wilson, in clay image-making, with the Devil as guide. The purpose was to kill all the male children in a local landowner's family. First, John Taylor brought home some clay, and his wife broke it into very small pieces, sifted it with a sieve and poured water on it in the Devil's name. Then they fashioned images in the likenesses of the landowner's sons. As they made each image they learned the magic chant from the Devil. Then they all fell upon their knees, their hair over their eyes, their hands lifted up and looked steadily at the Devil and said the words three times. The figure, according to Isobel, "had all the parts and marks of a child, such as head, eyes, nose, hands, feet, mouth, and little lips." They then put each image in the fire until it was as red as a coal. The image was roasted on the following days, one part at a time. If it did not break, the witches believed that the death of all the male children would ensue, and the image would last one hundred years.

If the witches wanted milder sport, such as only to make the wind blow, they would take a rag of cloth and wet it, and take a beater and say three times over:

I knock this rag upon this stone,
To raise the wind in the Devil's name.
It shall not lie till I please again.

When they wanted the wind to die down, they would dry the rag and say:

We lay the wind in the Devil's name.
It shall not rise while we like to raise it again.

Isobel Gowdie admitted that the witches had no power of rain, but said they raised the wind whenever they pleased. These witches went often to the fields of those they wished to do harm, in order to make thistles sprout where corn had grown before. They believed that their own land would become richer thereby. Isobel Gowdie described one enchantment of the land: With the Devil leading, the members of the coven marched up and down with a tiny plough drawn by toads, with traces made of grass and a ram's horn as the blade. Up and down they went, the head of the coven holding the plough, exhorting the Devil for the fruit of that land, and wishing that thistles and briars would grow there.

The witches also went to the fields for another purpose —shooting. But this shooting was done with elf arrowheads, which had been shaped by the Devil, then turned over to elf boys for shaping and trimming and pointing. When the Devil gave the arrowheads to Isobel and the other witches, he would say:

Shoot these in my name
And they shall not go whole hame.

When the witches shot the arrows, they would say:

I shoot yon man in the Devil's name,
He shall not win whole hame.
And this shall be always true,
There shall not be a bit of him on lieiw (alive).

The witches had no bow to shoot the arrows with, but "spang them" from the nails of their thumbs. Sometimes, Isobel said, they missed their target, but when the arrows hit, "be it beast, man, or woman, it will kill."

Isobel described with zest her first arrow-shooting venture with the coven witches: They went again to a field and there shot a man "and he presently fell to the ground, upon his nose and his mouth." The Devil gave Isobel an arrow and had her shoot a woman in the field. She did so and the woman fell down dead. Isobel and the other witches dried up a cow's milk or a sheep's milk when they wished. Other times they took away the strength of a person's ale. Then they did the Devil's work with one Alexander Cumming's dyeing vat. They took threads of different colors of yarn, cast three knots on each thread in the Devil's name and put the threads in the vat, and thus took away the strength of the dye so that poor Alexander Cumming could dye things only black.

On other occasions they went down to the shore to harass the fishermen. Before the fishing boats came in they would say:

The fishers are gone to the sea,
And they will bring home fish to me.
They will bring home intill the boat,
But they will get out of them but the smaller sort.

Then, when the boats came in, the witches would either steal or buy a fish. They believed that by their magic the fishermen's fish would turn to "froth."

Isobel Gowdie went about through the years visiting the "downie-hills, and got meat there from the Queen of Faerie." Sometimes, in a good mood, she would use her magic for a good purpose, perhaps to cure a fever. She had a regular charm that she believed would rout out "quaking-fevers, the sea-fevers, the land-fevers, and all the fevers that ever God ordained." After she had said her charm three times the fever would go "out of the heart, out of the back, out of the sides, out of the knees, out of the thighs, from the points of the fingers to the nebs of the toes, out fall the fevers."

Many assumed that Isobel Gowdie was suffering from some type of insanity to make such confessions in court about her witch activities. But all the indications were proof that she was indeed sane. Though she testified a number of times, she never wavered from her basic account and she never contradicted herself. She did, however, express great sorrow and repentance for her crimes. On one occasion, she said: "I have done so many evil deeds, especially killing of men . . . I deserve to be riven upon iron harrows, and worse if it could be devised."

Whatever happened to Isobel Gowdie? The records do not say.

B. GILLES DE RAIS

One of the most notorious cases of witchcraft, and one of the most gruesome, concerned a wealthy Frenchman, Gilles de Rais, who lived in the fifteenth century. What a sordid later history he had, compared to his glorious early life when he was the comrade and protector of Joan of Arc! Gilles de Rais fought at Joan's side in her battles because he believed in her cause. He performed so gallantly that when King Charles was crowned, Gilles de Rais was made a Marshal of France. He soon tired of court, however, and retired to his castle of Tiffauges, where he lived in luxury. Knights, captains and squires dressed in brocade and velvet were his bodyguards. His chapel was rich and ornate. The vestments for the services were jeweled, the silks woven with threads of gold. There were lavish tapestries and candlesticks of gold.

Gilles de Rais had hundreds of guests. He loved rare spiced foods and rich wines, and served such fare to his guests.

He had trunks full of precious manuscripts, many of which had been decorated for him by a famous illuminator. In truth, Gilles de Rais lived so well that finally his money began to dwindle. So much of his land had to be sold that his family became concerned and a council order forbade him to dispose of any more property. It was at this time that he turned to the occult and magic to refill his coffers. He came under the spell of a famous occultist, Gilles de Sille, a priest. Then he applied to Jean de la Rivière, a sorcerer. And finally, a certain du Mesnil persuaded Gilles to sign in blood a document giving all to the Devil. Soon, de Rais came under the power of Francesco Prelati, a dishonored Florentine priest and sorcerer.

Then a series of murders began. The wizard Prelati said that Satan demanded the blood of children and that if he had such blood he would reward de Rais with riches. The first child to be killed was a young boy who had been lured to the castle. For the next eight years, young boys and girls kept disappearing, all sacrificed by de Rais who sought to please the Devil, not only so he would regain his lost wealth, but also to obtain supernatural powers. According to some estimates, more than 800 children met their death at his hands.

Eventually, rumors of Gilles de Rais's witchcraft and murders began to circulate, and they came to the ears of the Bishop of Nantes. After a month of inquiry, armed men were sent to the castle, and Prelati and his followers were taken.

At the trial, Gilles de Rais was accused of the murders and of practicing witchcraft and Satanism. He replied with foul words. Then, on the third day of the trial, he seemed transformed. Bent and trembling, he made a full confession of the horrible things he had done. So ghastly was his recital that those present shuddered and a veil was put over

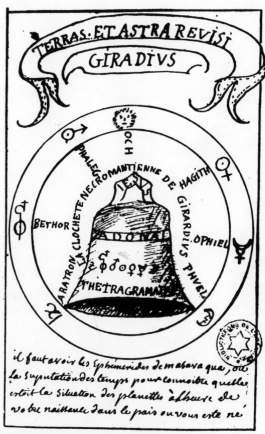

Necromantic bell of Girardius

the crucifix that hung above the bishop's throne. In the end, Gilles de Rais was declared guilty of witchcraft, Satanism and heresy, among other crimes. He was sentenced to death and was hanged. A stock of brushwood and tar beneath the gibbet was lit and the flames rose up. His body was then removed from the fire, before it was consumed, and buried in the churchyard nearby.

C. THE CHELMSFORD WITCHES

The Chelmsford district in England in the sixteenth century was a great center of sorcery. So many witches confessed that the Chelmsford witches achieved notoriety. Pamphlets were written about them, and the accused were tried before distinguished courts. The queen's attorney, a judge of the Queen's Bench and a parish rector were among those who listened to the testimonies.

Elizabeth Francis, the first to be examined, claimed that she learned the art of witchcraft at the age of twelve from her grandmother. She had renounced God and had given of her blood to Satan. Satan, in turn, gave her a white spotted cat which she fed bread and milk. She kept the cat in a basket and called it Satan.

Elizabeth's first request of the cat was that it arrange affairs so that she would become rich. The cat, she testified, promised that Elizabeth would have what she desired. Her first desire was sheep. The cat, in a strange hollow voice, promised her the sheep and sure enough, eighteen black and white sheep appeared in Elizabeth's pasture land!

Next, Elizabeth Francis wanted a certain Andrew Byles, a man of some wealth, for her husband. The cat promised she would have him, but arrangements went awry and Andrew did not marry Elizabeth. She then willed the cat Satan to lessen Andrew's worldly goods, which it did. But Elizabeth was not satisfied and asked the cat to kill Andrew. The cat touched him and Andrew died.

The cat Satan then set about getting another husband for Elizabeth. This was accomplished, but the marriage was not happy. Elizabeth then asked the cat to kill her child, which was done. But still Elizabeth was not satisfied. Her husband, Francis, annoyed her, so she willed the cat to make her husband lame. The cat did this by getting into Francis' shoe as a toad one morning. As he went to put on the shoe, Francis touched the toad with his foot and was startled. Elizabeth told him to kill the toad and he did, and suddenly he was afflicted with lameness.

Finally, after fifteen or sixteen years of this, Elizabeth tired of the cat. She went to her neighbor, a poor woman of about sixty-five called Mother Agnes Waterhouse, and gave her the cat. Elizabeth instructed her, as she had been instructed so many years before by her grandmother, to call the cat Satan and give him bread and milk and her own blood. The cat had grown used to blood, for every time

Witchcraft y᷎ practice of deluded minds,
Where grace is wanting soon admission finds.
With golden promisses of life & wealth.
The Tempter takes unwary souls by stealth.
In this his seeming clemency appears,
That he will give them back a leafe for years.
But y᷎ expir'd, how dismall is their end.'
And case, when he a Feind shall for them send.
Tis death to think of mending when too late,
And glories given for so vile a rate.
As power to hurt another, & to sin
With greater freedom, from controll within.
That Laws divine, & humane, should not be
The least restraint, to their impiety.
That reason should be set aside, & death
Become their choice, when they resigne their breath
That piety should be of no esteem.
Nor Faith in him, that only can redeem.
All their conceited pleasures come to this,
When yelling they discend y᷎ grand Abyss.

Witch and her cat

he had done something for Elizabeth she gave him a drop of blood by pricking herself in one place or another. (Wherever she had pricked herself, a red spot remained.)

Poor Mother Waterhouse! She was tried as a witch in July, 1566, before a justice and the queen's attorney. She confessed that indeed she was a witch. She had a cat and willed it to destroy many of her neighbors' cattle. In addition, she had sent her cat Satan to a nearby tailor, a man named Wardol, with whom she was at odds. Satan was to destroy him and all his goods. But in spite of a number of attempts, Satan had to give up because Wardol was so strong in his faith that Satan could not hurt him.

One day Mother Waterhouse's daughter, Joan, went to a neighbor's house where twelve-year-old Agnes Brown lived and asked for a piece of bread and cheese. Agnes said that she had none, and that she did not have the key to the milkhouse door.

Joan was angry with Agnes. When she got home she remembered that her mother often went around the house calling Satan. So Joan went up and down the house and called Satan. A black dog appeared and asked what she

Witch drawing milk from an ax handle

wanted. Joan became frightened and said she wanted Satan to make Agnes Brown afraid. The black dog asked what his reward would be. Joan promised a red cock, but the dog did not want that. He asked for Joan's body and soul, and because she was afraid, Joan gave up her body and soul to the dog. She testified in court that she had heard Agnes Brown had been made afraid.

Then Agnes Brown was called upon to testify. She said that on the day in question she was churning butter and there appeared some creature like a black dog with a face like an ape. It had a short tail, a chain and a silver whistle about its neck, and a pair of horns on its head. It brought the key of the milkhouse door in its mouth, and asked for butter. Agnes was afraid and said she had none. The dog creature unlocked the door and went into the milkhouse, and when it came out it told Agnes that it had made butter for her. Agnes told the court that the creature came back many times, and that there indeed had been butter in the milkhouse after its first visit. Agnes also incriminated Mother Waterhouse as the owner of the creature.

Mother Waterhouse was promised by the queen's attorney that if she would summon the creature, she would be let out of prison. But she could not do so; she asserted that her power over the creature was gone. The climax of the trial came when Mother Waterhouse was asked if the cat had sucked of her blood. She replied, "Never."

Then the jailer lifted up the kerchief on her head and there, for all to see, were the spots on her face and one on her nose.

Two days later, Mother Waterhouse wailed and repented and asked the mercy of God just before she was hanged.

D. THE NORTH BERWICK WITCHES

One of the most amazing groups of witches was to be found
in Scotland in 1590. These were the North Berwick witches
who plotted against the life of King James. By the time
the trials were held, over seventy persons had been implicated. At the end of the confessions and trials a number
of the witches were hanged.

It was completely by accident that the conspiracy
came to light. Undoubtedly it was led by the Earl of
Bothwell, an enemy of the king.

Here is the tale: David Seaton, deputy bailiff of a small town about ten miles from Edinburgh, had a maidservant, Gilly Duncan. It was rumored about the town that Gilly was performing miraculous cures on the sick and lame. Her reputation for curing maladies grew, as did the number of her absences at night from her master's house. David Seaton became suspicious. Was he perhaps harboring a witch in his house?

Such cures, he knew, could not be effected without resort to some supernatural power. He questioned his servant. She gave him no answers, but he persisted—even with torture. Her fingers were abused and her head was wrenched with a cord, but Gilly Duncan would not confess. Then a diligent search was made to find a witch's mark on her, which would be certain proof that she was a witch. Such a mark was found in "the forepart of her throate." Immediately, Gilly Duncan confessed that all her doings were done by the "allurements and enticements" of the Devil, and that they were done by witchcraft.

What a reaction this confession provoked! Gilly Duncan was sent to prison, and there she accused one person after another of being a witch. Chief among these was Agnes Sampson, the eldest witch of them all, and Dr. Fian, a schoolmaster. Those accused were cast into prison until the facts could be ascertained by the authorities.

Agnes Sampson was brought before the court, which consisted of the king and lesser nobility, to confess her crimes. As much as the king tried to persuade her, Agnes denied all charges of witchcraft. She was whisked back to prison and there endured the usual torture meted out to witchcraft suspects. In the search for the witch's mark, all of Agnes Sampson's hair was shaved off. She was tortured with ropes, but still maintained she was innocent. Then, what was taken to be a witch's mark was found! (A mole or a pimple could be a witch's mark.) She confessed to being a witch and consequently implicated all those previously mentioned by Gilly Duncan.

Agnes Sampson was brought again before the king. This time, she had much to tell about the activities of the witches. On All-Hallow E'en, she said, she and 200 other witches went to sea in sieves, drinking wine as they floated to the church of North Berwick, where they danced and sang. Gilly Duncan played the music on a small instrument, called a "Jew's trump." They all sang:

> Cummer, go ye before; Cummer, go ye;
> If ye will not go before, cummer, let me.

The king was so fascinated by this testimony that he sent for Gilly Duncan to perform for him on the strange instrument, which she did.

At the church in North Berwick, Agnes said the Devil, in the likeness of a man, spoke against the king. (It has been believed that the king's archenemy, the Earl of Bothwell, acted as the Devil in the witches' meetings.) After the dance and the speech and feasting, the witches—possibly drugged—took themselves off "in their sieves in the sea."

The king was much interested in Agnes Sampson. He was not fool enough to be unaware that he had many enemies. Francis Stewart, the Earl of Bothwell, for example, would succeed to the throne of Scotland if James died without leaving children. The king was impressed by Agnes Sampson's statement that the Devil hated the king, "by reason the king is the greatest enemy he hath in the world." But then Agnes began to elaborate too much on parts of her confession.

So unusual and fantastic did these events seem (sailing

on the sea in sieves, for instance) that King James finally blurted out that they all seemed to be complete liars. Agnes was to convince him otherwise, however. She took the king off to one side and whispered to him the words that he and his wife had spoken to one another on the first night of their marriage. King James was astounded, for Agnes' words were correct, and he believed that "all the Devils in hell could not have discovered the same." Now King James gave more credit to Agnes Sampson's testimony.

Agnes Sampson admitted that she was involved in a plot to kill the king. She said that she had taken a black toad and hung it up by its back feet for three days and collected the venom as it dropped into an oyster shell. She kept the venom until such time as she could get some piece of the king's soiled linen. A shirt, a handkerchief or any piece of cloth that the king had soiled would do. Agnes had hoped to get such linen from one of James's attendants, but was unable to do so. If she had she said, she would have bewitched the king to his death, "as if he had been lying upon sharp thornes and ends of needles."

The witches had also taken a cat and christened it and thrown it into the sea, hoping thus to wreck the king's ship on its return to Scotland with his new bride. They also made a wax image of the king, so that he would languish as they burned it. All, of course, to no avail.

The meeting of the witches on October 31 had indeed been called, Agnes testified, to discuss some way to harm and, if possible, to kill the king. The Devil, from his pulpit, had urged all the witches to be good servants to him and he, in turn, would be a good master to them. He made a frightening appearance. Agnes described him: "His face was terrible, his nose like the beak of an eagle, great burning eyes, his hands and legs were hairy, with claws upon his hands and feet." The Devil may well have been the Earl of Bothwell. His connection with the witches was well-known at the time and Agnes, in her confession about the wax image, had implicated him.

Agnes said that she had made the figure, which was wrapped in linen cloth. It was given to the Devil at the coven meeting. The Devil recited over it, then passed it back to Agnes and she, in turn, gave it to the next person, who gave it to the next. As the witches took the image, they chanted the Devil's words: "This is King James the Sixth, ordered to be consumed at the instance of a noble man, Francis Earl Bothwell."

Perhaps the Earl of Bothwell did believe in magic. Later, when he was poor and an exile in Naples, he wrote against Christianity and urged Christians to "abjure Christ and your baptism" and "stand fast with me—I shall give you what you desire."

As for Agnes Sampson, she was executed.

Gilly Duncan had placed the fate of death upon the schoolteacher John Fian, known as Dr. Fian, when she testified that he was the Devil's register, or secretary. Dr. Fian was thrown into prison, where he was tortured with ropes. He confessed nothing. Then verbal persuasion was used, again to no avail. Finally, Dr. Fian was put into a crushing instrument called "the bootes." Still, he did not confess. Other witches suggested that his tongue be searched. Under his tongue were found two pins thrust in as far as their heads, which had prevented him from confessing. The pins were removed and the victim was released from the bootes and brought before the king, where he confessed to being a witch.

Dr. Fian said that by the use of "sorcery, witchcraft and devilish" practices, he had bewitched a gentleman who lived near Saltpans, where the doctor kept a school. This gentleman was enamored of a certain lady in whom Dr.

The imprint of the Devil's claw

Satan makes his future disciples tread upon the Cross

Fian was interested. Fian bewitched him into a lunacy that lasted an hour. To prove his guilt, Fian had the gentleman brought before the king. Indeed, the gentleman seemed bewitched. He gave a great screech, bent himself double, then leaped so high that his head touched the ceiling of the court chamber. He cavorted about so that help had to be called to control him. His hands and feet were tied; then suddenly, he came to himself. When asked by the king what had happened to him, he replied that he had been in a sound sleep.

Dr. Fian signed a confession of his guilt of witchcraft, and was taken to a solitary room in the prison. There, he acknowledged that he had indeed led a wicked life. He renounced the Devil and vowed to lead the life of a Christian thereafter.

The next morning, he had strange news to tell. He said that during the night the Devil, all in black and with a white wand in his hand, had come to him and demanded to know whether Dr. Fian would continue in his service, according to his first oath. Fian then renounced the Devil to his face: "I have listened too much unto thee. . . . I utterly forsake thee." To this, the Devil answered: "Once ere thou die thou shalt be mine." And with that, the Devil broke the white wand and disappeared.

Dr. Fian, confined in solitary, brooded about this visit from the Devil all that day. He called upon God and repented of his past. The next morning, he was gone. He had found some means to steal the key of the prison door and the cell he was in, and had fled to the area of his school. Eventually, the king's emissaries tracked him down and he was brought back to prison, and before the king for reexamination.

But Dr. Fian was a changed man. Before, he had freely given his confession of guilt and had even signed

Torture of the pincers inflicted on a sorcerer

such a confession. Now, however, he denied everything. The only explanation seemed to be that he had again made contact with the Devil and had pledged himself anew to serve him. He was carefully searched for a new witch's mark, but none could be found. The king realized that Fian was being extremely willful and stubborn, and ordered further torture.

This time, Fian's fingernails were pulled off with a pincers called a turkis, and under each fingernail two needles were thrust in and forced to full length. Still, he admitted nothing. He was again taken to the bootes, where his legs were crushed. Still, no confession was forthcoming. Everyone assumed that the Devil now had Dr. Fian fast in his hold. Fian repeatedly denied his earlier confession and said he had only made it out of fear of the pains he had endured. Now, however, he was being subjected to even greater pain and torture. Still, he denied his guilt. Finally, the king and the council decided that he must remain a "terror to all others thereafter that shall attempt to deal in . . . witchcraft, sorcery, conjuration, and such like." Dr. Fian was arraigned, condemned and sentenced to be burned. On a Saturday at the end of January, 1591, he was strangled and his body was placed in a great fire and burned to ashes.

E. LADY ALICE KYTELER

The first witch to be burned in Ireland was not the most famous witch of the time but rather, a pupil of one she described as the most skilled sorceress, the mistress and teacher of witches.

The pupil, Petronilla de Meath, was burned on Saturday, November 3, 1324. The teacher, Lady Alice Kyteler, a rich and influential lady, had been pronounced guilty of witchcraft the previous July, but escaped death by flight to England.

Satan gives the adepts a Black Book in exchange for the Gospels

Lady Alice Kyteler lived in Kilkenny with her fourth husband, Sir John Le Poer, at the time when the Bishop of Ossory, under commission of the Pope, was investigating heresies in his diocese. Much to the bishop's announced horror, he discovered that there were many sorcerers in the city of Kilkenny, and leading all the rest was Lady Alice, who was "with her many accomplices involved in various such heresies."

Prime among her accomplices were her son, William Outlawe, an influential banker; Robert de Pristol, a clerk; and Petronilla de Meath, a matron, and her daughter, Sarah. The charges against Lady Alice and the other sorcerers were very specific. In order to obtain their ends by black magic, they had renounced the Christian faith and had abstained from entering churches. They had sacrificed to the Demon live animals which they offered, at a crossroads, to a spirit named Filius Artis (or Robin, or Robert Artisson). This spirit was the familiar of Lady Alice. He appeared to her in various shapes: sometimes as a cat, sometimes as a large, black shaggy dog, or as a huge black man who had two tall dark companions carrying iron rods. It was charged that Robin was the source of all of Lady Alice's wealth and good fortune.

The witches were accused of seeking advice and answers from demons. It was said that they used the church for their nightly meetings, during which they held mock excommunications with lighted candles of wax "even against the persons of their own husbands, naming expressly every member from the sole of the foot to the top of the head, and at length extinguishing the candles with the exclamation 'Fi! Fi! Amen.'"

They were charged with preparing drugs, unguents and powders to cause love and hate, disease and bodily harm. They made these instruments by compounding such materials as herbs, spiders, black worms, scorpions and serpents.

Lady Alice was also accused by some of the children of her previous husbands of having killed those husbands by witchcraft in order to get their property. By the same means, it was now charged, she was causing her current husband, John Le Poer, to become ill. However, a maid-servant in the household warned him and he forcibly took from his wife the keys to her chests and boxes. In these chests, he found all the implements of sorcery: phials, concoctions and strange instruments. He packed up the evidence and sent it, under the care of two friars, to the bishop.

Lady Alice was further charged with having nightly meetings with the spirit Robin, and sacrificing to him "nine red cocks and nine peacock's eyes." In addition, a wafer of sacramental bread with the Devil's name stamped on it, instead of that of Jesus Christ, was found in her closet, and also ointment with which she greased a staff upon which she galloped about.

It was also stated that Lady Alice would go about with a broom in the afternoons and sweep the streets of Kilkenny "raking all the filth toward the doors of her son, William Outlawe" in order to attract money to him. As she swept, she would chant:

> *To the house of William my son*
> *Hie all the wealth of Kilkennie town!*

The bishop had made his investigation and had unearthed the vile evidence of sorcery. Now he must convict those accused. This would be more difficult than it first appeared, however. Cases of sorcery had always been dealt with in England by the secular courts, and the Church had had no jurisdiction in such cases.

The Bishop of Ossory was determined to handle the cases, however. He went to the government authorities and asked for a writ for the arrest of those accused. Heavy disputes between Church and government representatives followed, with the result that the bishop took matters into his own hands and called upon Lady Alice to appear at his court. She refused. The court met and passed a sentence of excommunication against her, and then charged her son, William Outlawe, to appear at a future date.

The government Seneschal of Kilkenny, Arnald de Poer, well aware of the influence and wealth of Lady Alice and William Outlawe, became furious at this turn of events and had the bishop seized and held prisoner in Kilkenny Castle. Matters became confused and complicated as the battle between the Church and the government raged.

After his release from prison, the bishop attempted to be heard at a secular court and was ordered ejected by the seneschal. The bishop persisted and read out the names of those accused of sorcery, and called upon the government to give them up to the Church.

Lady Alice, the chief offender, slipped away to England. William Outlawe finally appeared before the bishop's court, but attended by many armed supporters. No one dared arrest him, even after the charges against him were read out. Eventually, however, he was seized and imprisoned until he begged to be reconciled with the authorities.

The bishop finally pardoned William Outlawe after Outlawe publicly renounced all his heresies. For penance, he was to pay for a new lead roof on the cathedral and to fast every Tuesday until he made a special pilgrimage to a shrine at Canterbury.

Although poor Petronilla de Meath, an accomplice of Lady Alice Kyteler, fully confessed her evil deeds, it did not help her much. She had renounced the Christian faith, sacrificed to the Devil and consulted with demons, she said, as a pupil of Lady Alice, who had taught her the secrets of witchery. Petronilla declared that there was no more powerful witch in the whole world than Lady Alice. With Lady Alice, she had brewed philtres composed of adders, spiders, herbs and baby's brains. They had made ointments and had cast spells upon their enemies. Poor Petronilla was apparently proud of the powers and sorcery she and her mistress had used. She did not repent and was burned at the stake in the presence of a huge gathering.

Some of the others of that coven were burned, some were publicly whipped in the marketplace, some were banished and others were excommunicated.

But what happened to the Bishop of Ossory, who had

touched off the whole chain of events by his attempts to cleanse his diocese? He had accused Arnald de Poer, the Seneschal of Kilkenny, of heresy and had him excommunicated and sent to the dungeons of Dublin Castle. De Poer died while his case was being investigated. The Bishop of Ossory was eventually accused of heresy himself, and he fled to Italy.

F. ANNA MARIA SCHWAEGEL

Love was the undoing of the witch, Anna Maria Schwaegel, who was beheaded in Germany in 1775, the last witch to be executed in that country.

Anna Maria was working as a servant girl with a well-to-do family at Lachen. She developed a passion for the young coachman of the household who encouraged her and did all he could to hold her affection. But before they could be married, he said, she must renounce her Catholic faith and adopt his faith, which was Lutheran. This she did, yet the coachman deserted her and married another.

Anna Maria was disconsolate, disturbed by what she had done. She fled the household and wandered about the countryside as a beggar. She was found starving, with only a few rags clinging to her as clothing, and was taken to a Church asylum for the deranged. There, she fretted about her misdeeds, and one day confessed them to a friend. She said that not only had she forsaken the Church but that her lover was really a follower of Satan, and that she had attended Sabbats with him and had committed "unspeakable abominations at his behest." Time after time, Anna Maria repeated: "It was the Devil, under the form of this coachman, who betrayed me."

In due course, the superior of the home heard of Anna Maria's past and was horrified. She reported the case to the magistrate of the nearby town, Kemptem, and Anna Maria was arrested and taken into custody. At her trial, she repeated her story and added more facts. She had made compacts with the Demon, she said, and had assisted at many Sabbats. She had defiled herself. The judges listened and conferred. The only question was: Should she be burned or beheaded? The headsman was called in for Anna Maria Schwaegel.

G. THE WITCHES OF BURY ST. EDMUNDS

The witches of Bury St. Edmunds in Essex County, England, are interesting because their trials were to serve as models for later ones in America when the witch mania took hold there.

One spring morning in 1622, two widows, Amy Duny and Rose Cullender, were brought to the old town court-house adjoining the marketplace, to be tried as witches. The presiding judge was Sir Matthew Hale, one of the greatest lawyers of the seventeenth century. The charge was that the two women, one old and the other middle-aged, had bewitched Ann Durent, Elizabeth Durent, William Durent, Jane Bocking, Susan Chandler and Elizabeth and Deborah Pacy.

Samuel Pacy, father of the eleven-year-old and nine-year-old girls, was one of the chief witnesses. He said that his Deborah had been bewitched when Amy Duny came to buy some herrings and was refused service. As Amy turned away, muttering curses, Deborah was taken with the most violent of fits, "feeling most extreme pain in her stomach, like the pricking of pins. . . ." A few days later, her sister Elizabeth fell into convulsions, vomiting crooked pins and broad-headed nails. The girls cried out often in their fits: "There stands Amy Duny!" or "There stands Rose Cullender!" They swore that the two witches appeared before them and threatened that if they told what they saw

Possessed woman blaspheming at the beginning of a paroxysm

Possessed woman trying to throw herself out of the window

and what they heard, they would be tormented ten times more than before. Perhaps that is why when Elizabeth was called upon in court to testify, she was utterly speechless.

Ann Durent's two children were also taken with fits. On one occasion, when a doctor came to see one of the children, he advised Mrs. Durent to hang the child's bedclothes in the chimney corner and let them remain there all day. When she got them down in the evening, she was to examine them carefully. If there was anything strange in the clothes, it should be thrown into the fire.

When the clothes were taken down, "out there fell a great toad, which did run quickly up and down the hearth." The child caught the toad and held it over the fire with a pair of tongs. It flashed like gunpowder, exploded like a pistol shot and was seen no more.

The children's aunt then testified that the young ones, at her home, would sometimes "see things like mice, but which were not mice, running about the house." The aunt went on: "One day, one of them suddenly snapped one up with the tongs, and upon throwing it into the fire, it screeched out like a rat. At another time, a thing like a bee—but it was not a bee—flew into the face of the younger child; whereupon the child fell into a fit and at last vomited up a tuppenny nail with a big broad head to it."

The aunt declared that she herself "caught an invisible mouse, and throwing it into the fire it exploded like gunpowder. None besides the child saw the mouse, but everybody saw the flash."

Perhaps the accused would have been set free, for as one observer remarked at the time, in spite of the popular feeling against the two women "the evidence was not sufficient to convict the prisoners." In court, however, a distinguished doctor, Sir Thomas Browne, was observing the proceedings and was called upon to give his opinion. He said that "the fits were natural, but heightened by the Devil cooperating with the malice of the witches at whose instance he did the villainies." He therefore believed the persons were bewitched.

The court continued its inquiries. Charges were made that the two women had gone to buy some fish but objected to the price and indicated that the Devil should take the fishmonger and his money. The spell worked and the fishmonger was bewitched. A farmer testified that Rose Cullender had spoken sharply to him after his wagon had knocked a corner of her house. She threatened that his horses should suffer. Within a short time, his four horses died and he was taken with a lameness in his limbs. Others testified that the two women had caused poultry to die and a chimney to fall down.

A bewitched horse

The jury retired and, after half an hour, returned. The women, it decided, were guilty on thirteen indictments. They were urged to confess but would not do so, and were executed in the marketplace of Bury St. Edmunds.

H. ANTOINE OF SAVOY, FRANCE

The records of the trial, in 1477, of Antoine, wife of Jean Rose of a little village in Savoy, France, indicated that often those accused of witchcraft were tortured repeatedly, until the desired confessions were received.

Antoine had been denounced as an accomplice by a certain Massetus Garini before he was executed for witchcraft. She was brought for interrogation before the vice-inquisitor, who asked about her attendance at Sabbats, about her heresy and about her curing of children and animals by charms. Antoine denied everything and was condemned to torture. Finally, she agreed to confess and asked the mercy of the Church. After days of questioning, her history as a witch became clear.

Eleven years before the trial, she related, as she was coming from a chapel—upset because a certain man had seized three pieces of her land for a debt due him—she met Massetus Garini and told him of her troubles. Garini said there was a man who would give Antoine money to redeem her property if she would do what he told her to do. She agreed, and Garini called for her between nine and ten o'clock that evening and took her to a place where a Sabbat was in progress. There were many men and women dancing backward and enjoying themselves, Antoine related. She was frightened and wanted to leave, but Garini persuaded her to stay and see the Demon. The Demon was in the shape of a dark man called Robinet. He spoke in a hoarse, almost unintelligible voice, and promised Antoine gold and silver.

At the urging of the others, Antoine then renounced God and the faith, kissed the Demon on the foot and promised him a yearly tribute (which, she said, she had been paying ever since that time). The Demon marked her on the little finger of her left hand and gave her a purse full of gold and silver. When she opened the purse at home, she said, it was empty. He also gave her a stick and a pot of ointment. She was to use this stick often, anointing it and placing it between her legs as she said: "Go, in the name of the Devil, go!" Thereupon, she would be transported through the air to the Sabbat.

At the Sabbat, Antoine said, there were bread and meat to eat, although she just ate bread and cheese and drank wine. There was dancing, and for a time the Demon changed into the shape of a black dog. In answer to further

"The Sabbat" by Spranger

questions at the trial, Antoine described in great detail other Sabbats in other places. The next day she was questioned again, confirmed her confession and gave the names of thirteen persons she said had been at the various Sabbats. The following day she gave the names of four more persons and told of further activities, some of which are too horrible to relate.

Antoine confessed that the Demon had given them ointments to sicken people. Six years before, she had touched a four-year-old child with this ointment and the child had become sick and died within two weeks. Antoine and the others had also made powders to wreak evil on men and beasts. Antoine had killed four cows that belonged to a man who had beaten a goat of hers, and she had killed a cow of another man who had damaged her oats. The Demon had ordered the witches to do all the evil they could. In return, he promised that he would protect them from harm and see that none of them were arrested.

A few days after her testimony, Antoine was again brought to the courtroom. Again she confirmed all her wicked deeds and also reported that after the last questioning, the Demon had appeared before her in the shape of a huge man. He accused Antoine of renouncing him. She replied that she had, and that she was giving herself to God. Antoine then turned to her questioners, threw herself on her knees and begged for the mercy of God and the grace of the Church. The case was concluded and a time for sentencing announced. The records do not indicate Antoine's fate, but she was lucky if she escaped burning!

I. LAUTERFRESSER: MATHIAS PERGER

One witch's name—that of a man—was still used in Austria in the twentieth century to frighten children. The name is *Lauterfresser*. It was used by a man by the name of Mathias Perger, and inspired many tales and legends.

In 1645, when Perger was fifty-eight years old, he came to trial in the Tyrol, accused of consorting with the Devil and practicing sorcery.

He had spent his early life as a shepherd, but in recent years had wandered about, living in solitude. He had been taught to read by peasants and had taught himself to write. A bundle he carried was opened by the authorities and found to contain clothing, rosaries, pieces of bread, books of songs and devotions and a few other simple items. The books he possessed included some with charms for thieving and for controlling the weather, a book of astrology and an old, heavy Bible.

At his third audience with the judge and four jurymen, Perger had still not confessed to anything. When again asked about his actions, he told of various unimportant things. More than twenty years before, he said, he was with a peasant woman when a great storm arose, and she stopped the storm by hanging a bundle on a hedge stake. He said that in summer, a man should not wash on Friday, for if he did he would have to fear storms. He told of various other superstitious observances, but also declared that he had never caused storms.

Many hearings were held at which witnesses testified against Perger. Some said that he prophesied storms; others, that he was fond of wine, knew how to churn to make butter come, could read the planets, joked with serving women and children, foretold misfortune, quoted the Bible, often read the heavens and played evil tricks. Further, he was skilled in herbs and roots, and made snow.

After these accusations, Perger still denied that he practiced sorcery or had an evil spirit. The authorities decided to torture him. He was bound hand and foot and hoisted up to hang. More charges were made about his making hail and snow. The torture was repeated, and Perger hung three-quarters of an hour this time. He was then let down with the warning that only by confessing his guilt could he escape further torture. Again, he was hoisted up. Finally, after further examination with no results, he was put on a trestle for two nights and a day and was beaten when he fell asleep. His feet were squeezed together with irons, and his hands were tied tightly behind his back with a cord.

Finally, the torture was too much. Perger "confessed" that a woman at Landeck, whom he had met, might be a spirit. Her name was Belial and she had promised to marry him and make him rich. (This was more than twenty years before the trial.) She had given him a book, written in red, in which it was said that she was an evil spirit. He had met with Belial in the woods, and there he had renounced Christ and given himself to the Evil One. Belial drew some blood from his great toe and made him write with it.

Perger continued his recital of evil deeds. He had met some women who had taken him to a Sabbat, where he ate and drank. Belial had taught him to raise storms with a stone, hair and dust. He had seen twelve witches dance. One of them played a musical pipe and wore a feather and pointed shoes. At 6:30 in the morning, after Perger had confessed this much, he was released from the trestle.

The examinations continued, with further outpourings from Perger. He had a Devil's mark under his tongue. He went to many Sabbats, he said. Sometimes, the Devil appeared as a captain on horseback, with red insignia, sometimes as a pilgrim. At the dances, there was food: fowl, pork and lamb. Yes, he said, he had caused storms. He had caused a great one two years before by throwing dust and a woman's hair into water. Years before that, he went on, he had caused vines to freeze, using the same items, together with pieces of pine and bits of metal. Belial had helped him, and there had been rain, wind and snow, and all the fruits were destroyed.

He had turned himself into a bear for nine weeks, he said, after Belial had given him a skin that made him seem a bear. As a bear, he had killed five or six oxen and had eaten the best parts before giving back the bearskin. Belial had given him a yellow ointment with which he could transport himself whenever he wished. But Belial seemed to turn against him when he refused to damage fruit or make bad weather to destroy vines. She had seized him by the throat and tried to strangle him. On and on went Perger's recital to the judges. Finally, he was taken back to his cell, and because he feared Belial, he asked for holy water.

At the next session, Perger was asked to name all those he knew who also practiced sorcery. The names came tumbling forth. The old shoemaker had a witch's mark behind his left ear. Another taught sorcery. Another was a witch; another, a wizard with a mark under his left armpit (this man had a Demon named Stix). All those accused by Perger were brought before the judge and jurors for examination. They testified about storms, said they had seen bears kill oxen, and told of all sorts of events.

Perger was summoned again, and suddenly denied his confession. He was threatened with the ordeal of the red-hot iron plates, and taken back to his cell. His trial had started in May, and it was now October. On October 12, insisting that he had nothing to do with demons, Perger was placed on red-hot plates. He immediately confirmed his original confessions. That morning, fearing the torture, he tried to suffocate himself.

The judges and jury finally had enough evidence. Perger had not only confessed his own evildoings, but he had also implicated many others as witches. The jurors assembled once again to decide on the verdict. Some of them first cast ballots to have Perger torn with pincers; but they abandoned that idea. Instead, he was carried to his execution and burned at the stake.

J. THE WITCHES OF PENDLE FOREST

The witches of lonely Pendle Forest, among the hills of
Lancashire, England, were a wild, wretched group. Elizabeth Demdike, an ugly old woman of about eighty, had
been acknowledged to be a witch many years before her
trial, along with nineteen others, in 1612. About fifty years
before, she had been persuaded to become a witch, she
said, by a boy in parti-colored clothes whom she had met
by chance near a stone pit in Pendle Forest. Since that
time, she had dedicated not only herself, but her children

and her grandchildren, to the service of Satan. She was the leader of one band of the Pendle coven witches. Her rival in witchery was a wretched old woman named Anne Chattox. Each sought to outdo the other in wicked mischief. The two families, with their followers, waged heated feuds.

Elizabeth Demdike's daughter and grandchildren had no hesitation about testifying against her or, as a matter of fact, against one another. One granddaughter, Alison, said that her grandmother had made her a member of the coven by giving her a large black dog that was her spirit. Alison said she had lamed a peddler through the magic of the dog. She said further that her grandmother had bewitched a small girl to death, and also a farmer's cow. Alison testified that her grandmother was always very busy at some kind of magic-making that would cause evil to others.

Shortly after the trials began, the magistrate had heard enough. He ordered Elizabeth Demdike and three other women to be taken to Lancaster Castle. The witches were really disturbed now. The coven was summoned for a meeting at Elizabeth Demdike's house, Malking Tower. Here, the Pendle witches plotted as to how they might rescue Mother Demdike from the castle. They thought of killing the governor and jailer and blowing up the castle. They came to no definite decision then, however. Instead, they sat down to a dinner of "beefe, bacon and roasted mutton," after which they agreed to meet at a future date to solve the problem of Mother Demdike. Before such a meeting could take place, however, there were more arrests and a great deal of new evidence.

Mother Demdike's daughter, Elizabeth Device, and her children were then examined. Nine-year-old Jennet's testimony was most incriminating. Jennet, herself, was not bewitched, it was determined, but her evidence was introduced to incriminate her mother. Jennet said that she knew her mother was a witch for she had seen a spirit come to

"The Witches" (detail) *by Hieronymus Bosch*

her mother in the shape of a brown dog, which her mother called Ball. Ball and Elizabeth Device had destroyed three neighbors by witchcraft, she said.

But Jennet did not stop there. She described the meeting at Malking Tower, named those who were present and then gave detailed evidence against her brother, James. James, in turn, told about the evil deeds and teachings of his grandmother who, before going to prison, had asserted that her familiar had appeared to her in the likeness of a brown dog who forced himself to her knee "to get blood under her left arm."

The names of increasing numbers of prisoners were brought up at the trial. Anne Chattox' sins had been no less than Mother Demdike's. Some years before, she had killed John Device, the son-in-law of Mother Demdike, by witchcraft because he had not paid her the yearly tax he had promised if the Old Chattox promised not to harm him or his family.

Anne Chattox had also caused Robert Nutter's death by witchcraft. She then caused the death of Anne Nutter, who earlier had laughed at her. She also made John Morris' child ill by putting sharp pins in a clay image.

Alice Nutter, of the family stricken by Anne Chattox, was a lady of taste and breeding who possessed great wealth. Now she was implicated in the sorcery. Elizabeth Device accused her of having assisted Mother Demdike in bewitching a man to death.

Charges and countercharges flew, and the judges now had ample evidence to convict a number of persons as witches and, hopefully, to rid the area of those serving Satan. After the trial, ten persons were hanged. Among these were Old Chattox and her daughter; and Elizabeth Device and two of her children, Alison and James. As for Mother Demdike, she died in prison.

K. AMERICAN WITCHES

The witches of America became famous throughout the world largely because of the madness that seized the little settlement of Salem Village in 1692. During the previous years, belief in witches had persisted in the New World, encouraged always by reports of witchery in England. A number of witches had been hanged. There had been, however, no concerted hunt like the one that washed like a wave over Salem Village.

Witch-hunting in America received its first powerful

"There is a flock of yellow birds around her head."

impetus when, in 1688, the highly respected Cotton Mather was called in to study the strange fits of the children of a Boston family named Goodwin. Cotton Mather had already established a reputation for being heaven's messenger in routing out and destroying those doing the Devil's work.

One day, the Goodwins, a very pious family, were disturbed when they thought their washerwoman was stealing some of the family linen. When this was suggested to the servant, the old woman roundly cursed the family. Immediately, the Goodwin children fell into fits: Their limbs became disjointed. They went deaf and dumb and blind, by turns. Their tongues were pulled out by unseen spirits and then, as quickly, were let go and rebounded with a snap. Mr. Goodwin, highly distraught by what was taking place, called the clergy of the town in to pray and fast for the household. Cotton Mather was sent for, and he came and observed what was happening. One of the bewitched children would suddenly fall into a trance, jump into a chair and assume a riding position. The child believed that a witch had come for her on a horse.

There was nothing to be done but to accuse the old washerwoman. Arrested and interrogated, she denied her guilt, but she was sentenced to hang. Cotton Mather accompanied her to the scaffold, and she died on Gallows Hill, outside of Salem.

Mather now increased the tempo of his witch-hunting. He talked about the poor people who were molested by those of the unseen world. He deplored the presence everywhere of evil forces and called upon everyone to help him in routing out the witches. The populace became highly aroused about the presence and threat of the Devil's workers.

The Salem Village affair began in the household of Samuel Parris, a respected minister. His servants were a

West Indian slave couple, John Indian and Tituba, and it was only natural that on long winter evenings in 1691 and 1692, Tituba would amuse those gathered there with tales of Indian wizardry, barbaric rites, spells, dancing and evil spirits. She even hinted sometimes that she, too, knew the secrets of the spirits. Among those assembled to listen to the wild stories were Mr. Parris' nine-year-old daughter, Elizabeth; his eleven-year-old niece, Abigail Williams; Anne Putnam, aged twelve; and several other slightly older girls. Occasionally, a few of the married women would drop in to listen to the stories. Tituba had often described the dreadful fate of anyone cursed by a witch.

One day it was noticed that Elizabeth Parris, Abigail Williams and Anne Putnam were looking ill. They made antic gestures and loud outcries and behaved erratically. A physician was called in and diagnosed the cases as witchcraft. The distraught family called ministers in to pray, and the village folk chattered about the poor "afflicted children." The children had, indeed, achieved local fame. They were called upon to name those who had bewitched them and agreed that it was Tituba, Sarah Good and Sarah Osburn. Poor old Sarah Good and Sarah Osburn were two wretched, very old women who lived in want.

The three accused women were arrested. Sarah Good was examined first at the meetinghouse. She denied her guilt, but when the children were ordered to look at her, they seemed in torment. She continued to insist on her innocence. Finally, she said that Sarah Osburn was certainly the one who was hurting the children.

By this time, the children had adopted even more dramatic outward signs of their bewitchment. If one of the prisoners moved a limb, the children immediately cried out. If a hand was·raised, a child was being pinched. If a foot,

"The strange woman" and her spirits, A.D. 1621

then the children were being stamped upon. And always they cried out that they were being tormented by the witches. Sarah Good was finally hanged.

Sarah Osburn was then examined. She expressed her innocence, but was sent to prison in March, 1692, where she was heavily chained. She died there two months later.

Then Tituba was examined. She had seen that denial of guilt did not mean much to the examiners, so she assumed the role of the repentant guilty one. She *had* been in touch with the Devil, who appeared sometimes "like a hog, and sometimes like a great dog." But she asserted that Sarah Good and Sarah Osburn and two other women had hurt the afflicted children. So clever was Tituba in her defense that she was released without punishment.

But who were the other witches? The children were still severely afflicted, crying out in their pain. Who were the others who were tormenting them? The village began to wonder, and everyone began to look at his neighbor with suspicion. The panic grew, and more people were arrested. It soon seemed that the only way not to be accused was to become an *accuser*. More persons became afflicted. The first "witch" to be executed, Bridget Bishop, had been indicted for bewitching several persons. Her shape, it was said, had pinched, choked and bitten various villagers and had urged them to write their names in a book.

The accusations, arrests and trials continued. The afflicted children testified and performed their antics. Children even testified against their parents. One child of seven, Sarah Carrier, was asked, "How long hast thou been a witch?"

"Ever since I was six years old," she replied. She said that her mother had appeared before her in the shape of a black cat. "The cat told me so," she explained. She then confirmed the testimony of others that the Devil had promised her mother that she should be Queen of Hell.

The sheriff leading the witch up the broad aisle, her chains clanking

By July, 1692, five women, including Sarah Good, had been executed for witchcraft. Among those hanged on July 19 was Rebecca Nurse, who was a woman of about seventy, a respected member of the church, and of some social position. She was also ill and deaf. There seemed to be little proof that she was a witch. In fact, a paper testifying to her upright character had been signed by thirty-nine of her acquaintances and handed in to the authorities at the trial. The jury pronounced her not guilty, but pandemonium broke out in the courtroom as her accusers cried out and the afflicted children screamed. Benches were smashed and objects were thrown about. The jury retired, and then returned to the courtroom with their verdict—guilty.

Twelve-year-old Anne Putnam "cried out upon" the Reverend George Burroughs. Burroughs was a Harvard graduate; he had been pastor at Salem Village, but had left for another pastorate. In Boston one evening, as he was at the supper table with his family, the marshal arrived with a warrant for his arrest as "being suspected of a confederacy with the Devil." Burroughs was brought back to Salem and put in jail until he was brought before a special court.

Anne Putnam told a wild tale of how she had seen the apparition of Mr. Burroughs, who tortured her and urged her to write in his book, which she refused to do. She said that Mr. Burroughs' first two wives had appeared before her in sheets and with napkins about their heads and had said that he had murdered them. As if this were not enough, others came forward and said that Burroughs was the Devil of a witches' coven and had seduced many to join. He had been seen at a witch meeting, where they had "red bread and red drink." As the witnesses were testifying, they cried out that Burroughs was biting them, and the records say that there were seen on their flesh the prints of teeth.

The Reverend George Burroughs did not have a chance. He was executed in August, 1692, at Witchhill, along with John Proctor, George Jacobs, John Willard and Martha Carrier, whose daughter had said she turned into a cat. George Jacobs was a stout old gentleman who had vigorously denied any guilt. He had told the magistrates: "You tax me for a wizard; you may as well tax me for a buzzard. I have done no harm." But his brief speech did not help him any.

By September of 1692, nine more people had been sentenced to death. That same month, one Giles Corey was pressed to death. His wife, Martha, had been arrested months before on a suspicion of witchcraft. Mrs. Corey had repeatedly declared her innocence and her disbelief in witchcraft. Her husband was called upon to give evidence, and with horror he realized that what he was saying, in his zeal, would surely send his wife to the gallows. He refused to say more, and was arrested and charged with sorcery himself.

Giles Corey knew that if he was tried, he would be sentenced to death. To protect his property, which he had willed to his son-in-law, he vowed to remain silent. When asked if he was guilty or not guilty, he refused to speak. Thus, he could not be tried. But what a horrible sentence he thereby placed on himself! He was sent to a low, dark cell where he was stretched out upon the stone floor. Then he was loaded with a mass of iron that was increased in weight each day. A few crumbs of black bread and a sip of foul water were allowed him on alternate days. Finally, life left Giles Corey's body.

A few days after his death, eight others who had been sentenced were executed at Gallows Hill. As they died, the Reverend Nicholas Noyes, who had been watching, exclaimed sadly, "Alas! What a sad sight it is to see eight firebrands of hell hanging there."

By then, the prisons of Salem were full and so were those of Boston, Cambridge and Ipswich, for the mania had spread There was no more room to keep the accused. More executions were held on September 22 of that year, but they were the last. The tide was turning. A gentleman from Boston was accused of being a witch, but instead of being arrested or fleeing, he procured a writ against the accusers for defamation of character. The damages were set

An aged victim of superstition

at £1,000. Suddenly, his accusers no longer saw his shape torturing them!

In October, the wife of the Reverend John Hale, minister of a church in Beverly, was accused. This was too much for the sane minds. Mrs. Hale was a charming, pious and virtuous woman, beloved and idolized by those who knew her. The community rose to her defense and called the children who had cried out against her perjurers and liars. The witchcraft hunt was over.

The governor of the colony stepped in and forbade the special courts to try any more cases of witchcraft. He forbade the so-called spectral testimony to be considered evidence, and those who cried out that they were being tortured by witches could no longer be credited as witnesses.

During the year of the panic, twenty persons had been executed: nineteen by hanging and one by pressing. Two had died in prison, and eight were under condemnation when they were released.

Years later, a public confession by Anne Putnam was read out at the meetinghouse in Salem Village: "I was a cause, with others, of so sad a calamity . . . for which cause I . . . earnestly beg forgiveness of God, and from all those unto whom I have given just cause of sorrow and offense."

And here is the way one of the judges and twelve jurors expressed their repentance for what they had done: "We confess that we ourselves were not capable to understand, nor able to withstand, the mysterious delusions of the powers of darkness . . . we fear we have been instrumental, with others, though ignorantly and unwittingly, to bring upon ourselves and this people of the Lord the guilt of innocent blood . . . ."

The witch-hunt was truly over.

Bibliography

CAMPBELL, JOHN GREGORSON. *Witchcraft and Second Sight in the Highlands and Islands of Scotland*. Glasgow: James MacLehose and Sons. 1902

DARAUL, ARKON. *Witches and Sorcerers*. New York: Citadel Press. 1966

FIELDING, WILLIAM J. *Strange Superstitions and Magical Practices*. Philadelphia: The Blakiston Co. 1945

HOLE, CHRISTINA. *A Mirror of Witchcraft*. London: Chatto & Windus. 1957

HUGHES, PENNETHORNE. *Witchcraft*. Baltimore: Penguin Books. 1965 (First published by Longmans, Green, 1952.)

KITTREDGE, GEORGE LYMAN. *Witchcraft in Old and New England*. Cambridge: Harvard University Press. 1929

LEA, HENRY CHARLES. *Materials Toward a History of Witchcraft*. Arranged and edited by Arthur C. Howland. Vols. I, II, III. Philadelphia: University of Pennsylvania Press. 1939

MACKAY, CHARLES. *Extraordinary Popular Delusions and the Madness of Crowds*. L. C. Page & Co. 1932

MITCHELET, JULES. *Satanism and Witchcraft*. Translated by A. R. Allison. New York: Citadel Press. 1939

STARKEY, MARION L. *The Devil in Massachusetts*. New York: Alfred A. Knopf. 1949

SUMMERS, MONTAGUE. *The Geography of Witchcraft*. New Hyde Park, N.Y.: University Books. 1958

TINDALL, GILLIAN. *A Handbook on Witches*. New York: Atheneum. 1966

WICKWAR, J.W. *Witchcraft and the Black Art*. New York: Robert M. McBride & Co. 1926

WILLIAMS, CHARLES. *Witchcraft*. Cleveland and New York: The World Publishing Co. (Meridian Books.) 1959

Index

About the Author

OLGA HOYT was born in Columbus, Georgia. She has worked as an assistant news editor for the Office of War Information in Beirut, Lebanon; as a researcher for *Time* magazine in New York City; and as a news correspondent for the North American Newspaper Alliance in Europe.

For several years, Mrs. Hoyt was a columnist for the *Colorado Springs Free Press,* and was Editor of that newspaper's book section, which she established. She also wrote children's book reviews for *The New York Times* for a number of years, and did adult book reviews for *The Denver Post.*

Mrs. Hoyt has had two children's books published, and is completing a third. She also had an article she wrote on Ford Foundation grants to colleges published in the *Saturday Review.*

She and her husband—who is the author, Edwin P. Hoyt—live in an 18-room Vermont farmhouse with their three children. She does research and editing for her husband and, when she has time—and Vermont weather permits—enjoys gardening.